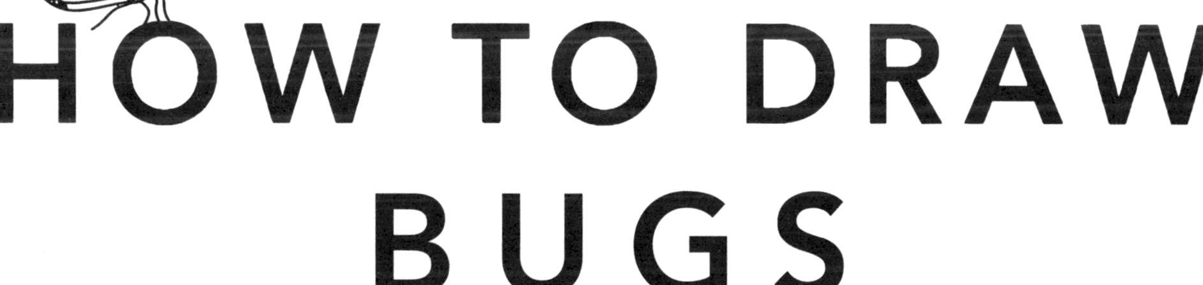

HOW TO DRAW BUGS
for kids

ALLI KOCH

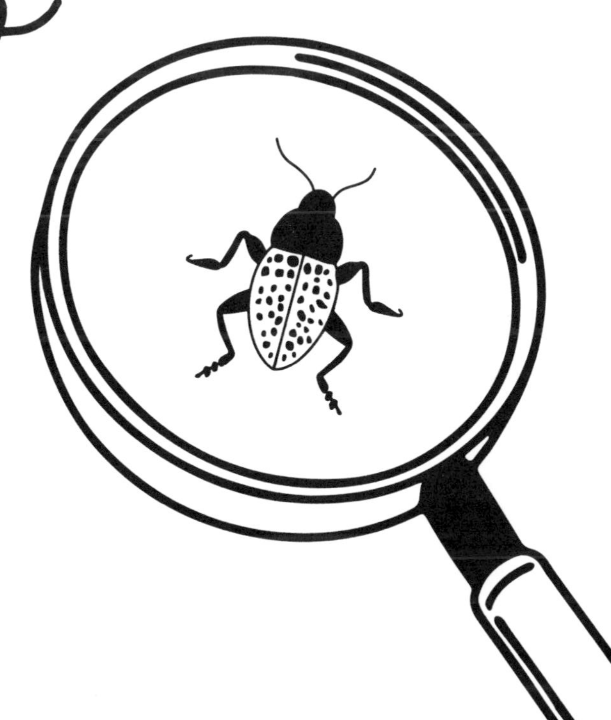

Paige Tate & Co.

Written and illustrated by Alli Koch

Printed in Colombia

10 9 8 7 6 5 4 3 2 1

ISBN: 9781963183726

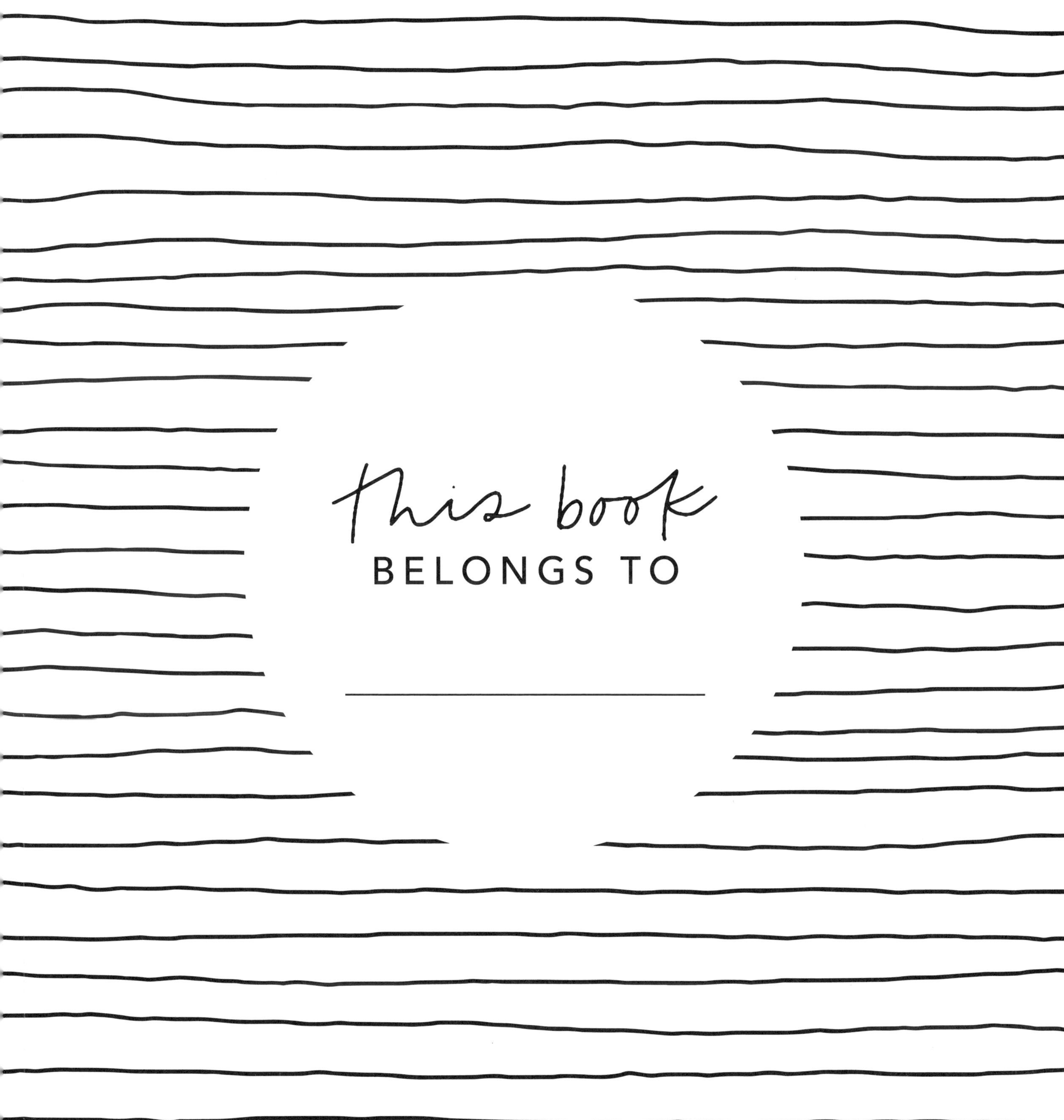

this book
BELONGS TO

INTRO — 5

TOOLS — 6

BREAK IT DOWN — 7

BUGS THAT FLY — 9

BUGS THAT CRAWL — 27

BUG THINGS — 59

CREATE YOUR OWN — 75

LET'S DRAW!

The nice thing about being an artist is that you can make the rules. Everyone has their own style, which is why your drawings will look different from someone else's. In this book, each project is broken down into easy-to-follow steps. My goal is to help you see the simple parts of what may seem like a hard thing to draw.

We will start with the most basic outline or guide and work our way up. You will start to see a pattern with each bug we draw, starting with simple guidelines, then breaking down "C" and "S" shaped lines, and lastly erasing the unneeded lines for the finished look. Don't forget to draw your lines lightly first so it is easier to erase them. My favorite thing to say when drawing is:

If it was perfect, it would not look handmade!

I cannot wait for you to get started.
Happy drawing!

TOOLS

The cool thing about art is that you can use any tool you want! Yep, that's right! You are the artist, so feel free to be creative. For this book, let's keep it simple. It's easy to learn using either blank sheets of paper or grid paper.

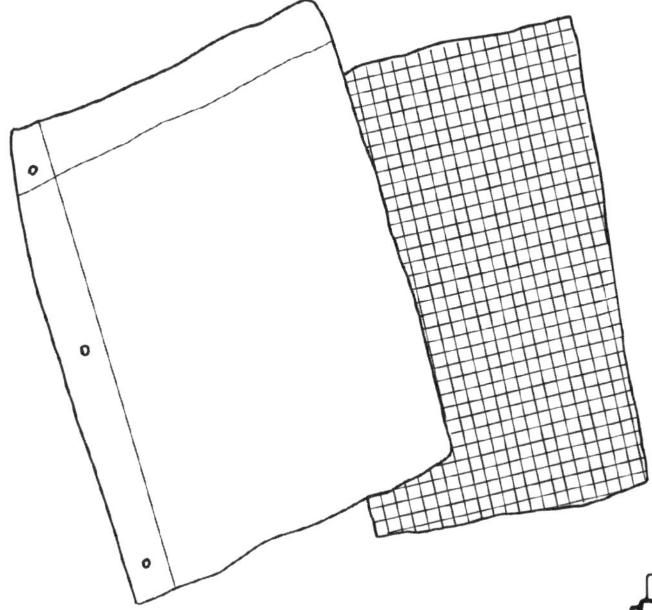

When you are learning to draw, you really only need a pencil and a good eraser. To follow the step-by-step instructions, draw everything lightly, then go over your lines with whatever tool you would like to use. You could use different pens, markers, colored pencils, or even crayons to add details to your drawings.

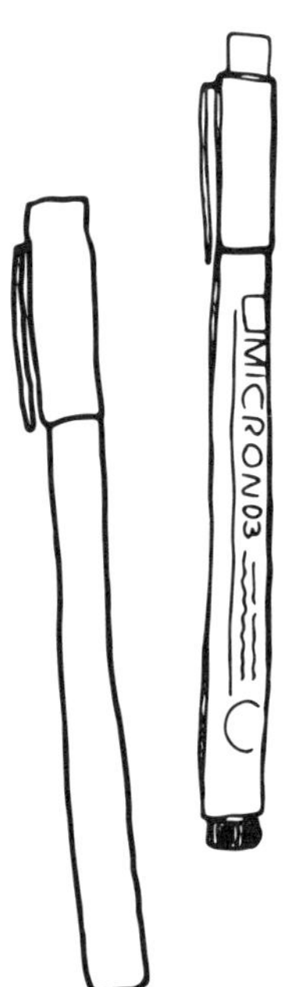

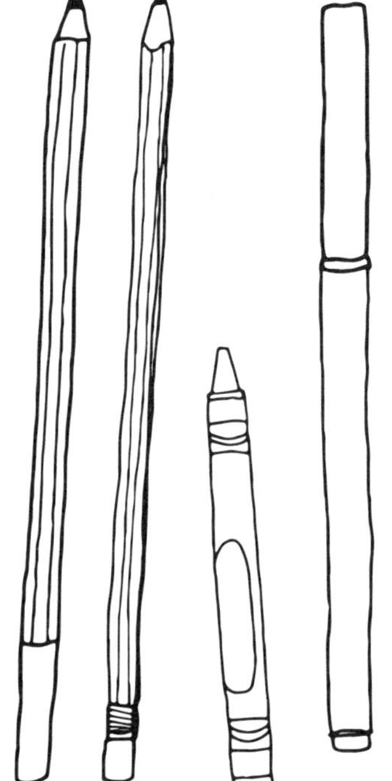

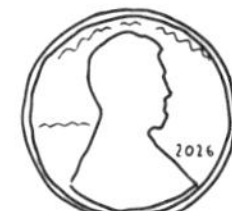

BREAK IT DOWN

Anyone can draw! If you can write your ABCs (which I am pretty sure you can do!), then you can draw everything in this book. Each project can be broken down into a bunch of "C" and "S" shaped lines. Almost anything that is round is two simple "C" shaped lines put together. An "S" shaped line is for when something has a dip or curvy line.

Most of the projects in this book are broken down into six or eight steps. What you need to draw in each step will appear as a black line; what you have already drawn will appear as gray lines. There are more than 35 bug-themed illustrations in this book for you to learn how to draw. The chapter dividers in this book are also bonus coloring pages that you can color!

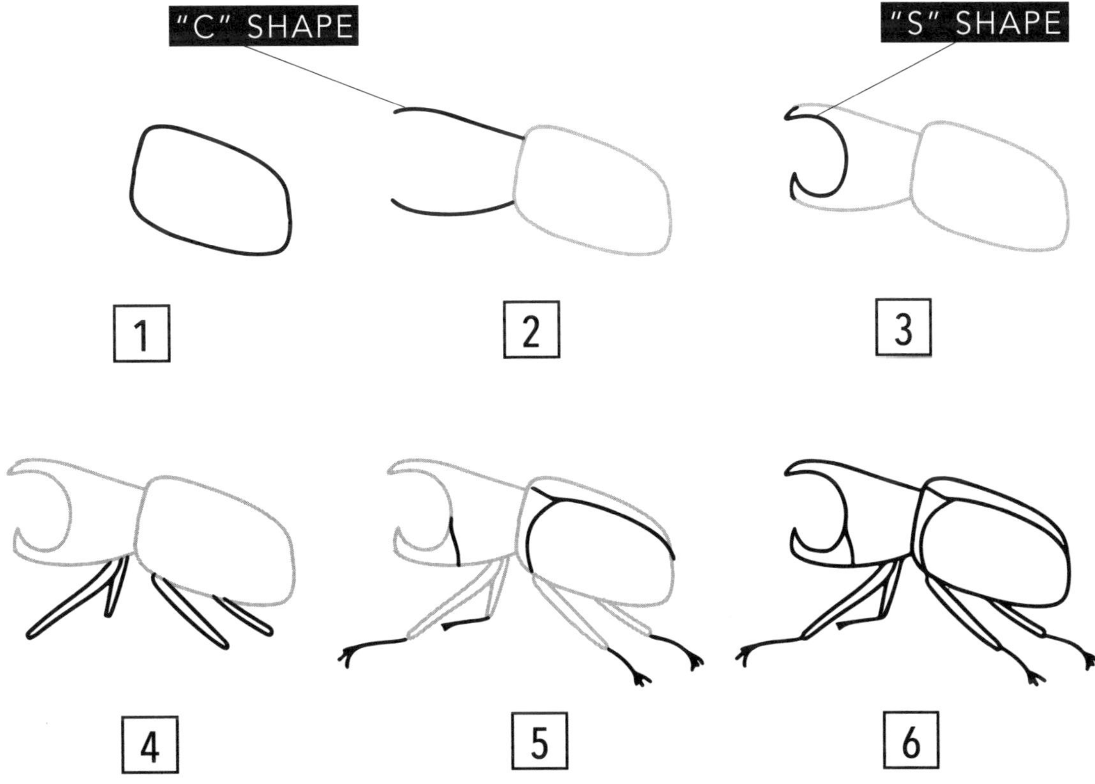

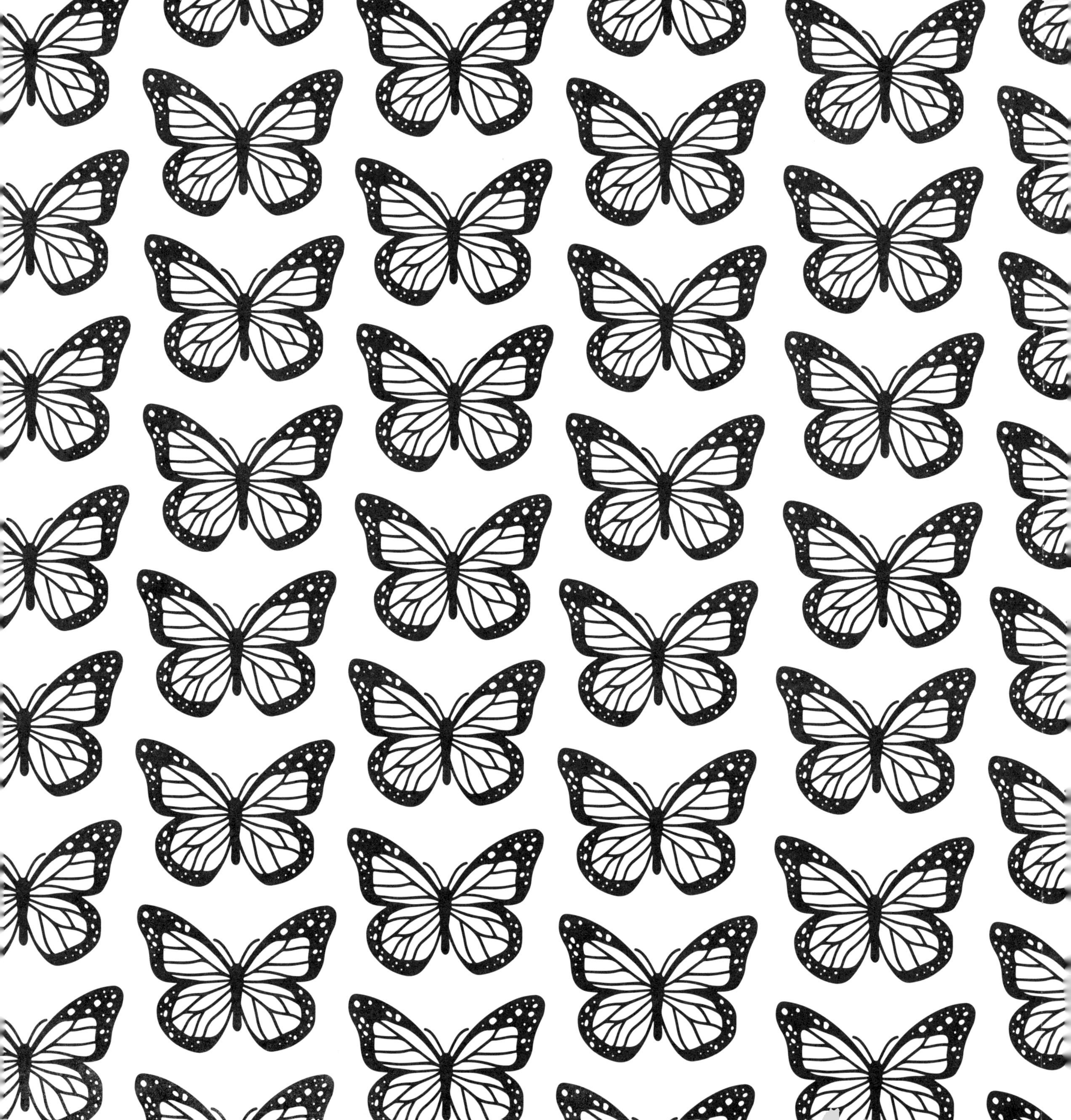

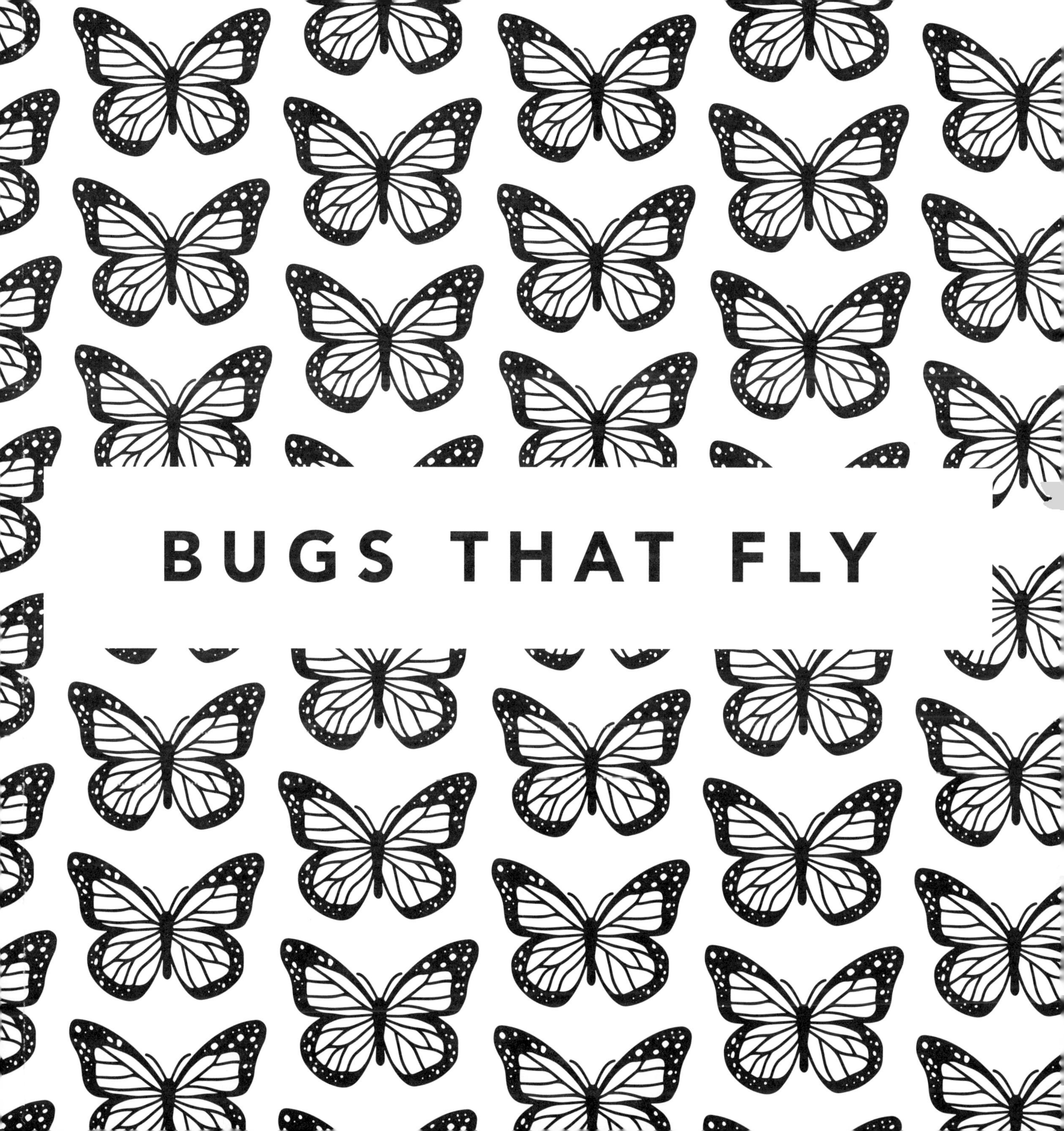

BUGS THAT FLY

LADYBUG

A single ladybug can eat more than 5,000 aphids in its lifetime.

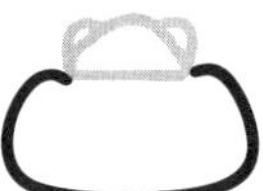

1

2

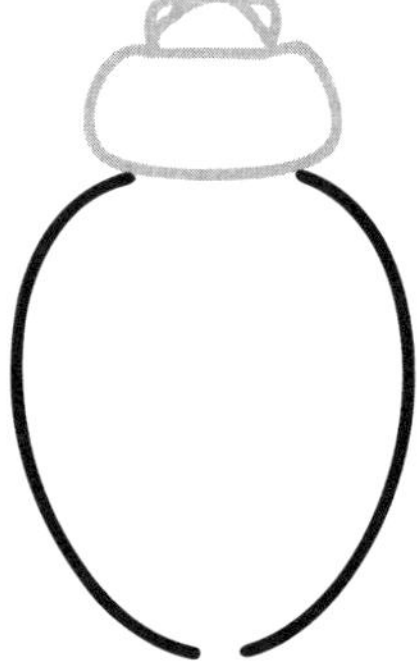

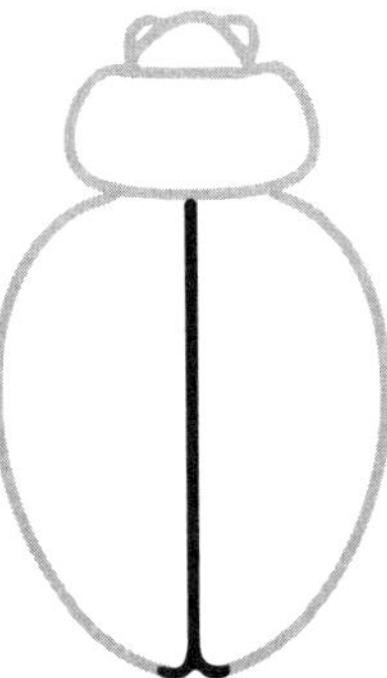

3

4

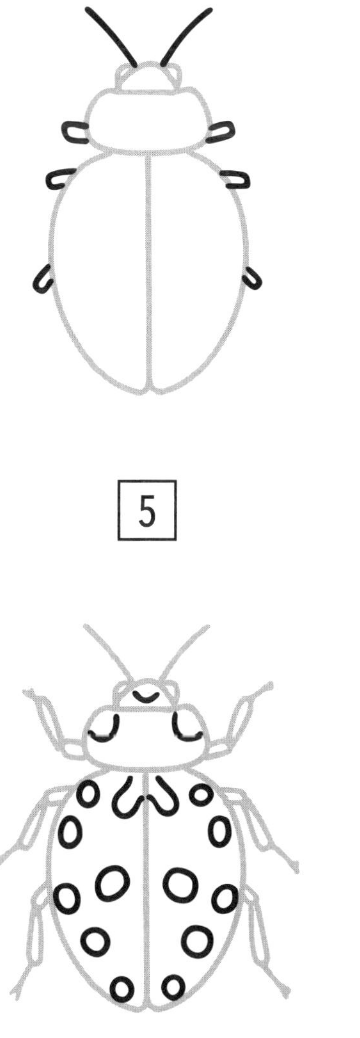

5

6

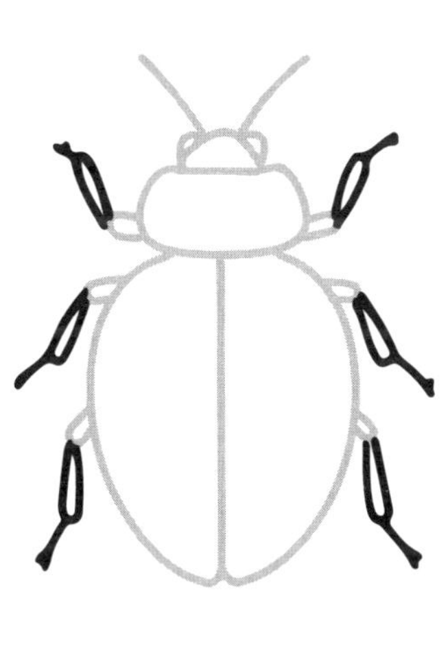

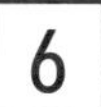

7

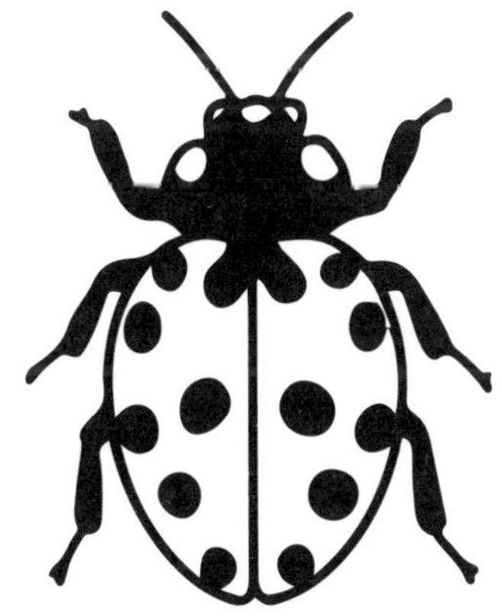

8

HONEYBEE

Honeybees communicate by dancing—a special *waggle dance* tells other bees exactly where to find flowers.

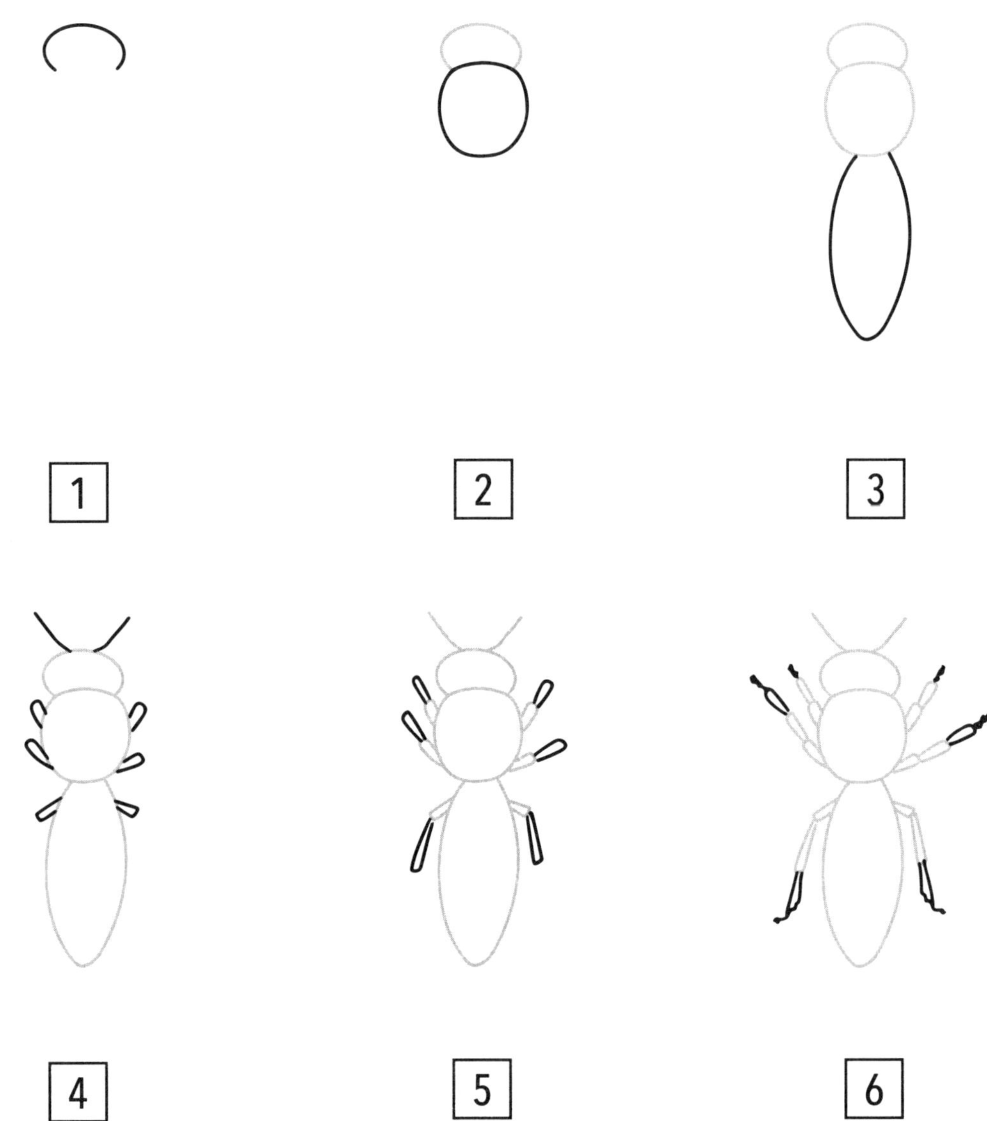

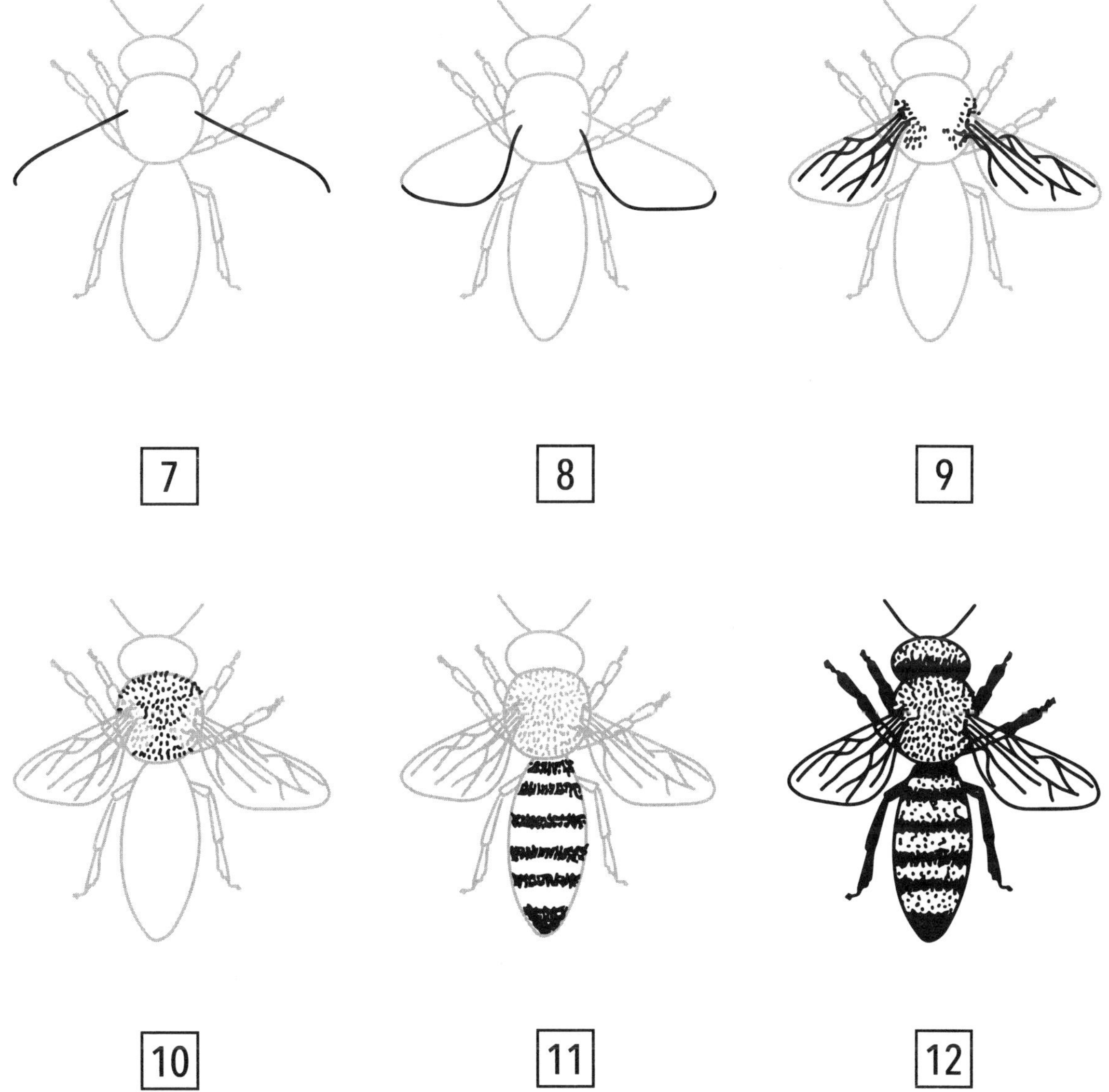

7

8

9

10

11

12

BUMBLEBEE

Bumblebees flap their wings about 200 times per second, which makes their famous *buzz* sound.

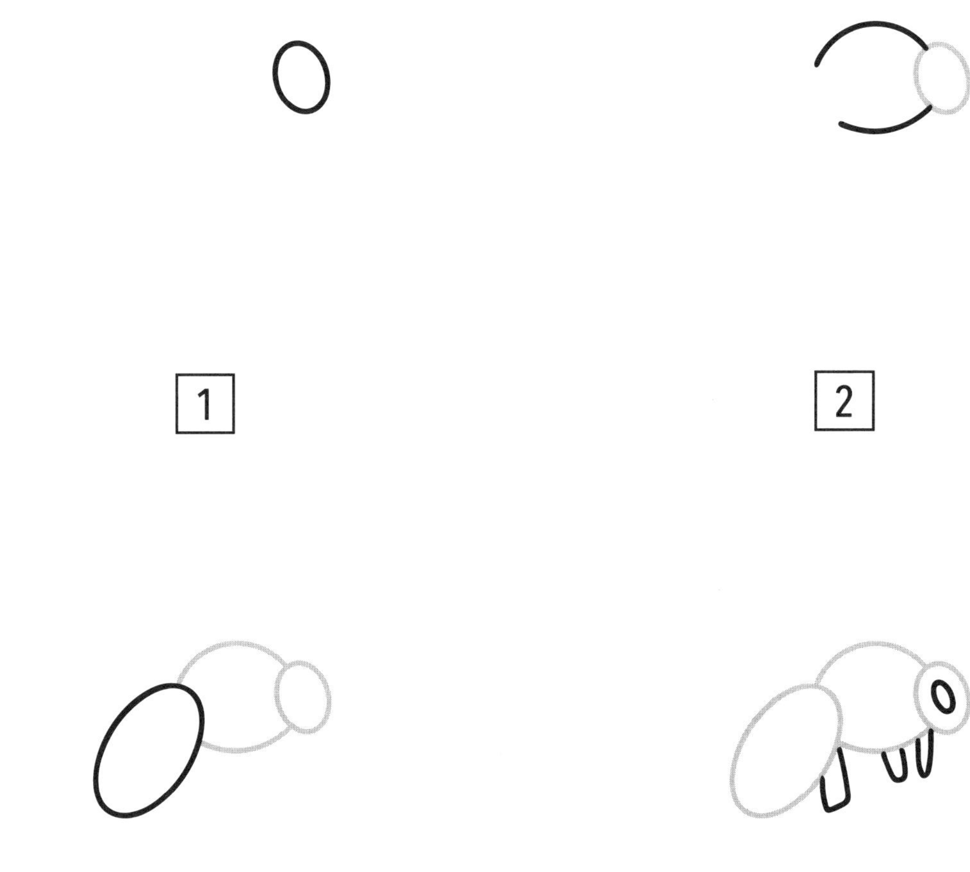

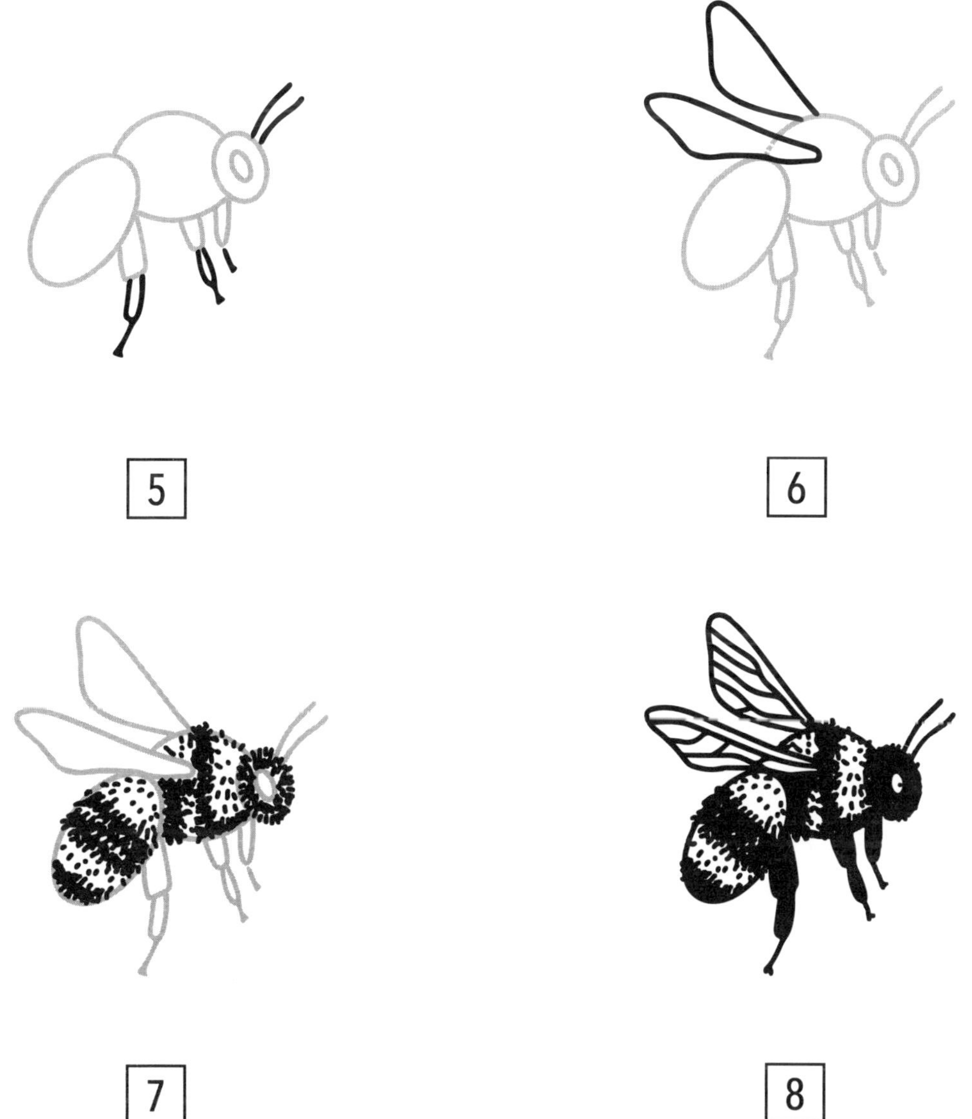

5

6

7

8

DRAGONFLY

Dragonflies can fly forward, backward, and sideways and some species can fly over 35 miles per hour.

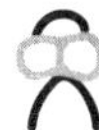

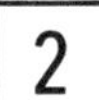

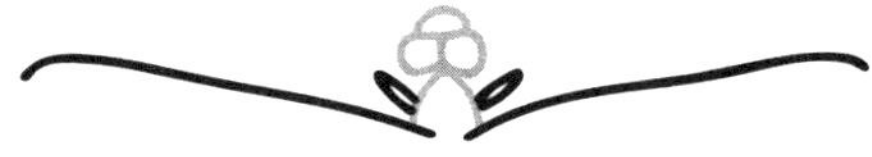

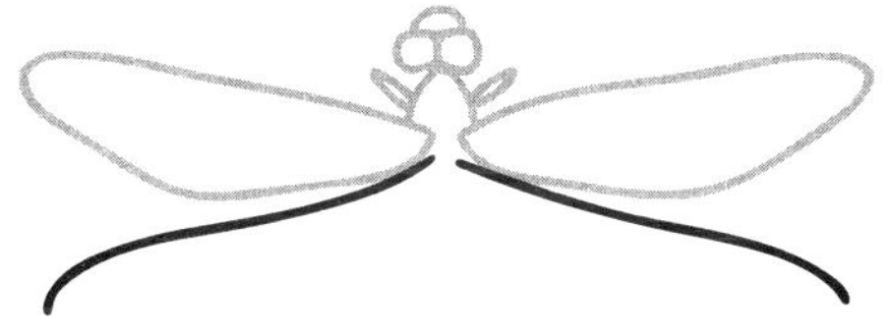

5

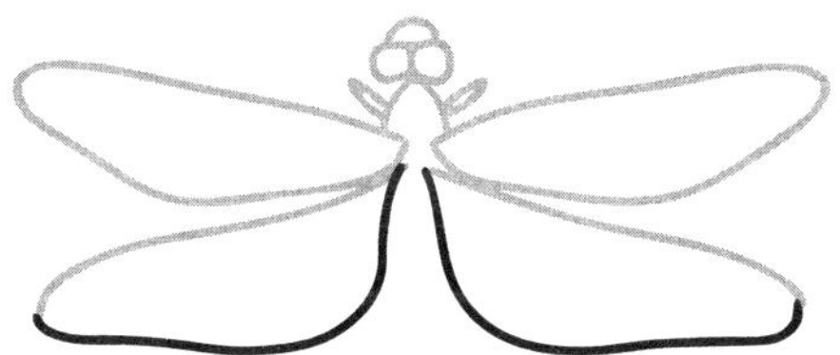

6

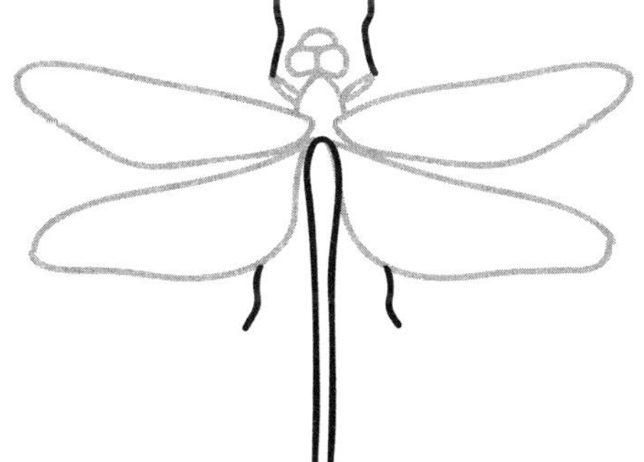

7

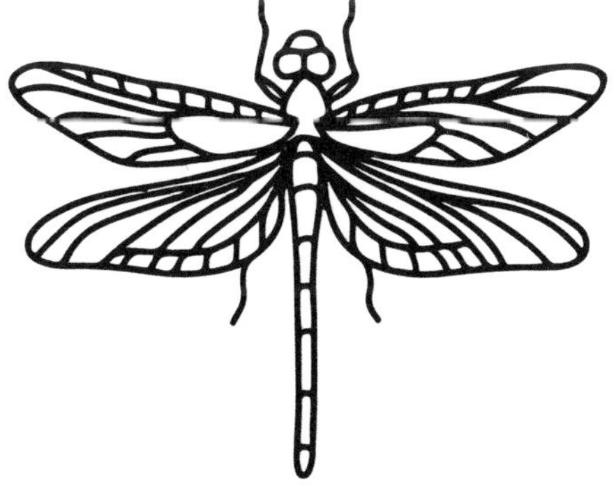

8

MONARCH BUTTERFLY

Monarch butterflies have the longest insect migration in the world.
Each fall, they travel up to 3,000 miles to reach warmer weather in Mexico.

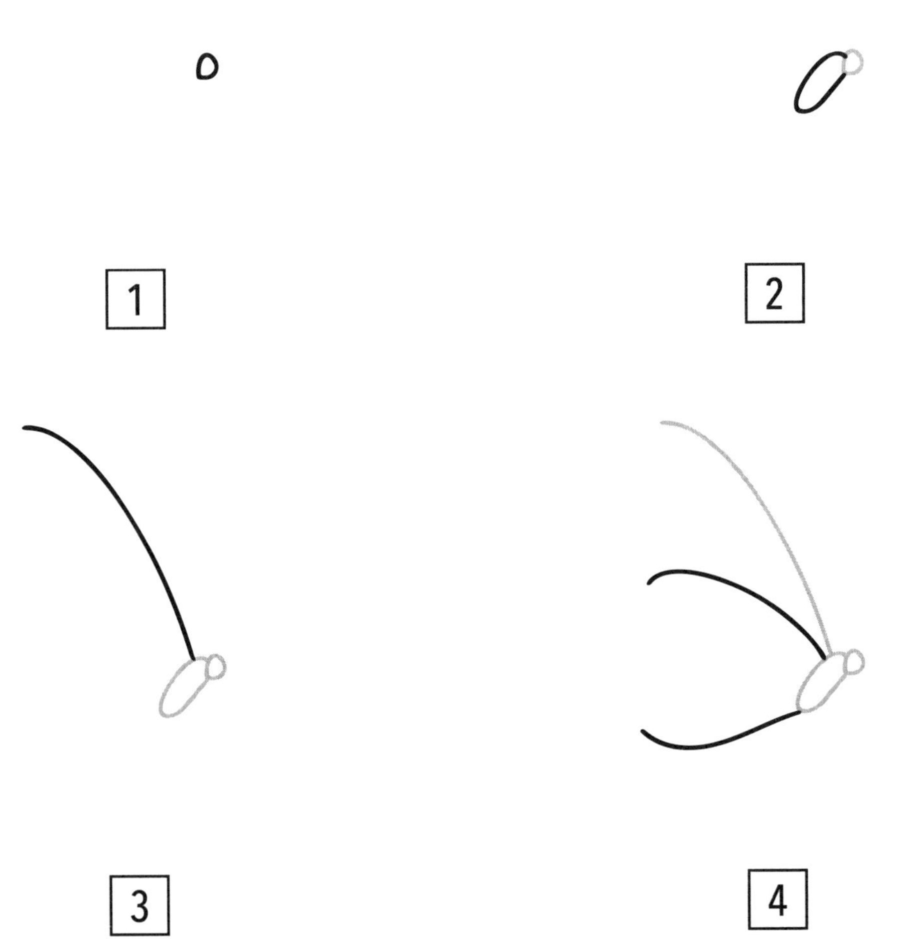

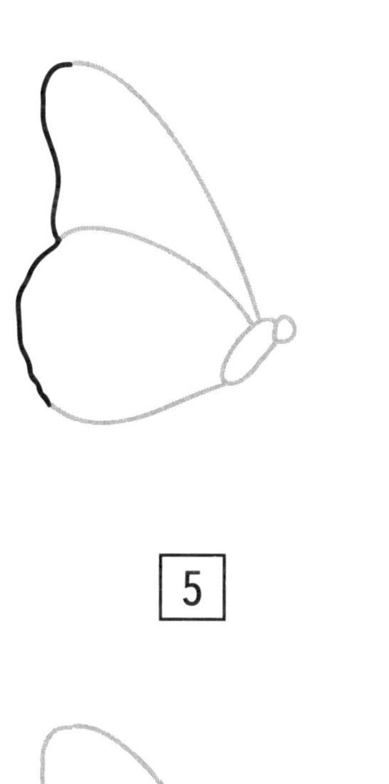

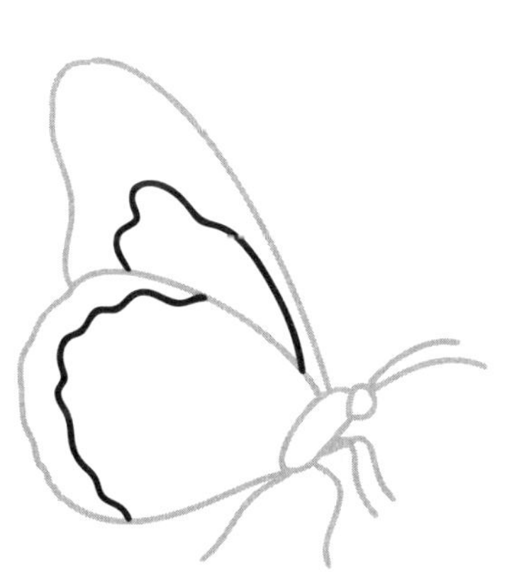

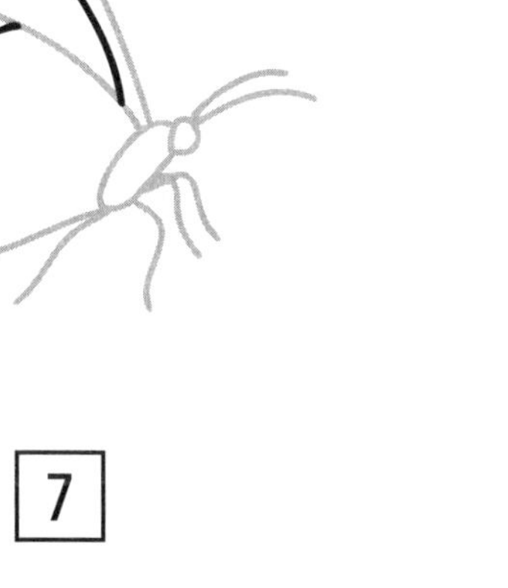

5

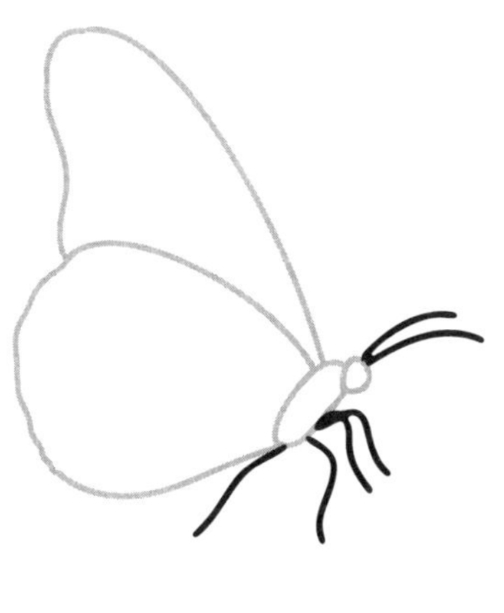

6

7

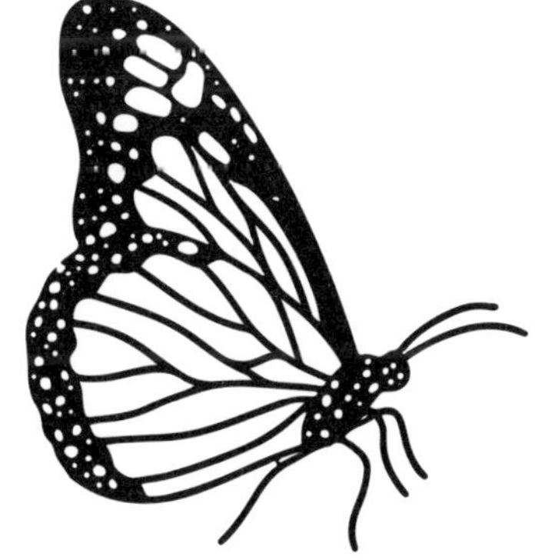

8

HUMMINGBIRD MOTH

Hummingbird moths flap their wings so fast they look like they are hovering in midair and most people mistake them for tiny birds.

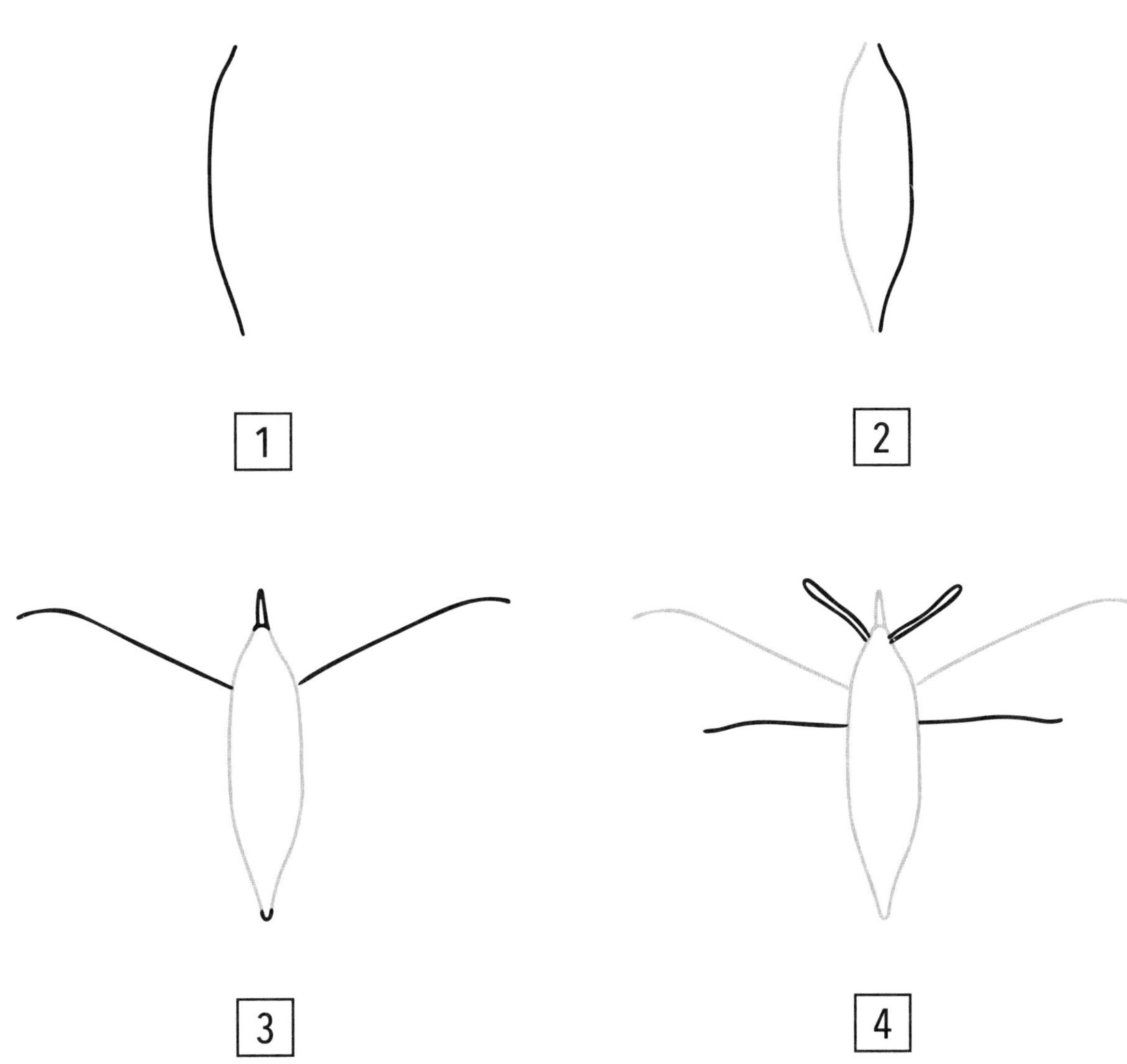

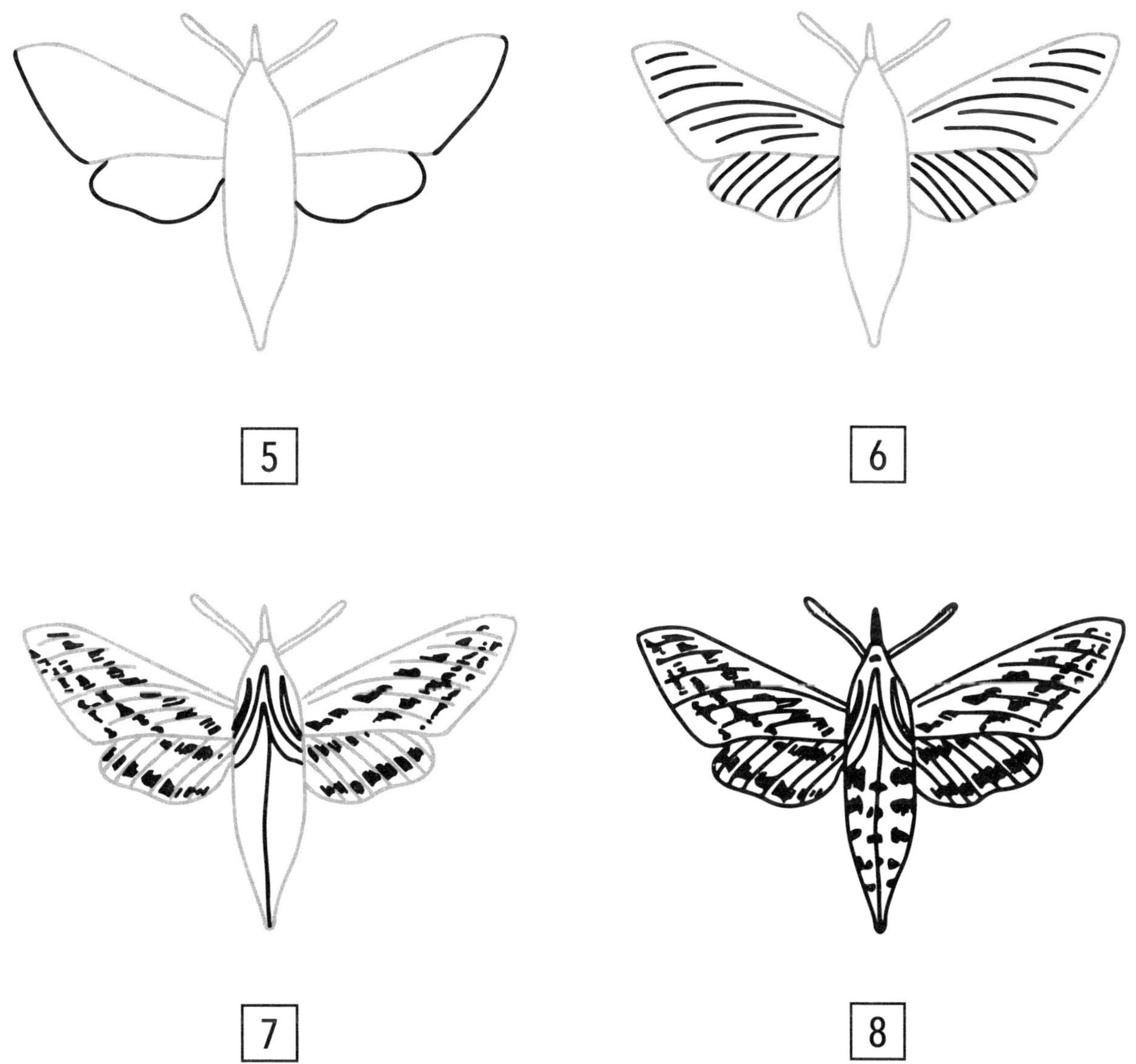

5
6
7
8

HOUSEFLY

Houseflies taste with their feet so when they land on food, they're actually sampling it.

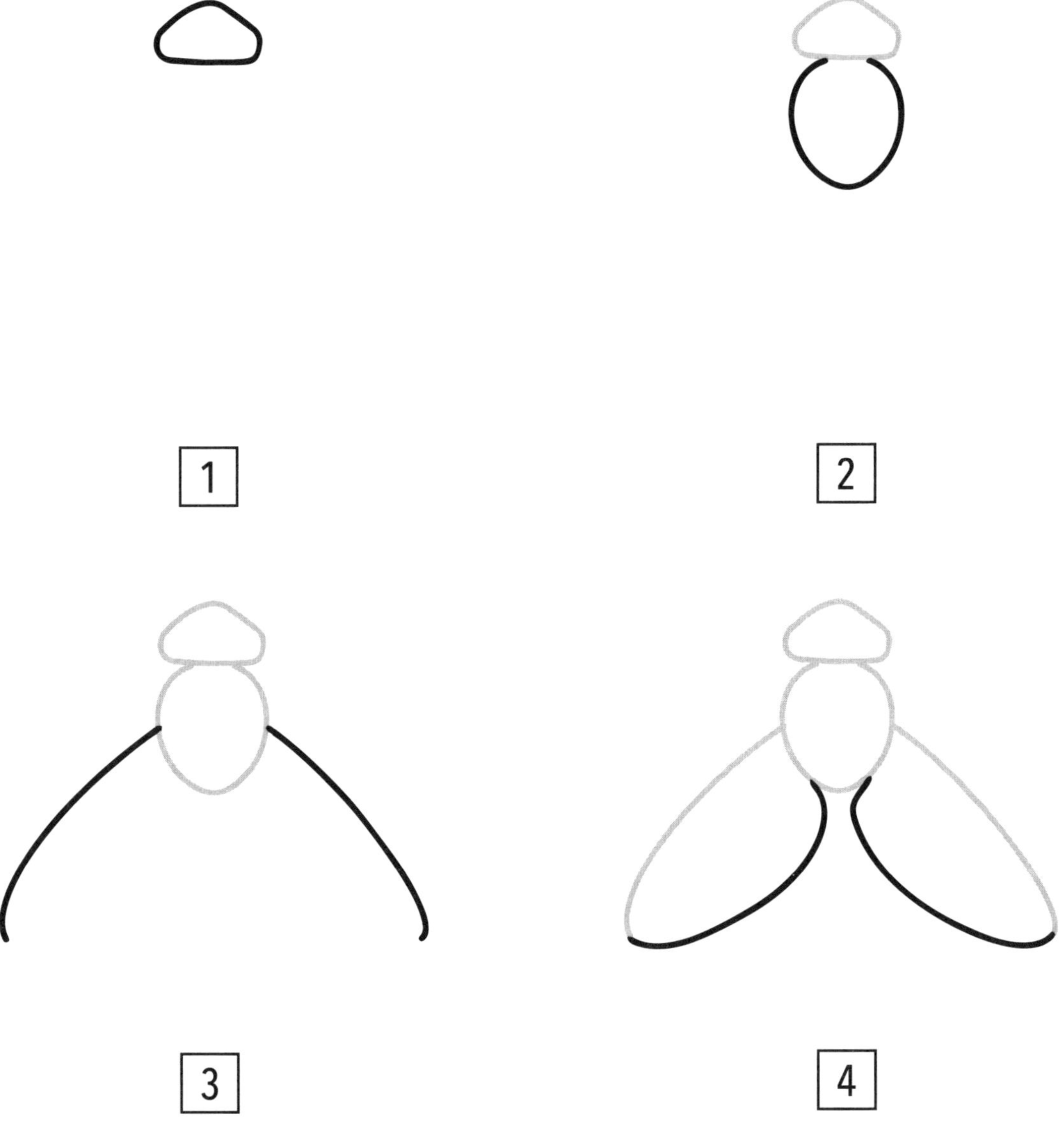

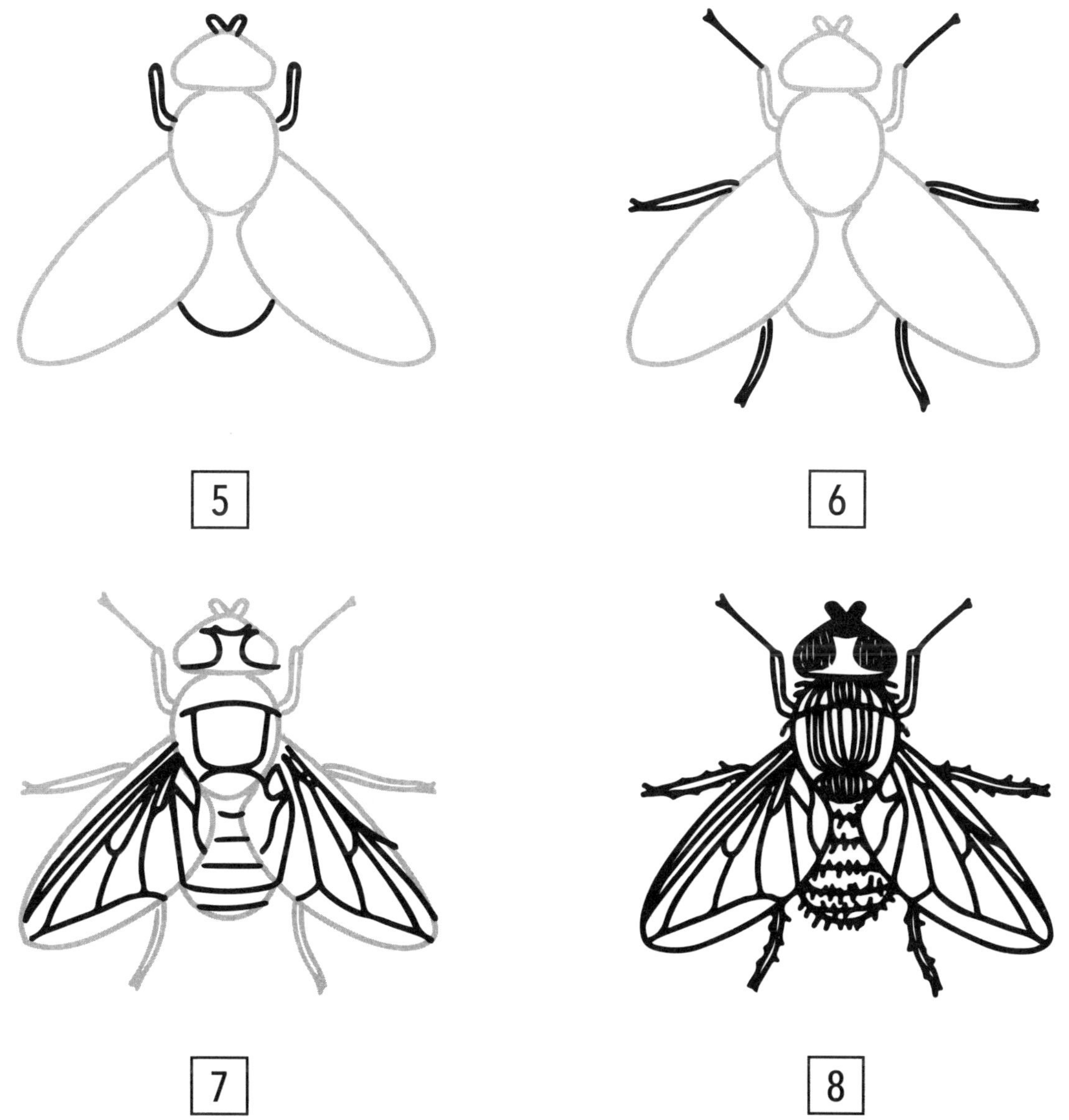

5
6
7
8

FIREFLY

A chemical reaction called *bioluminescence* causes fireflies to glow.
They use it to talk to each other and find mates.

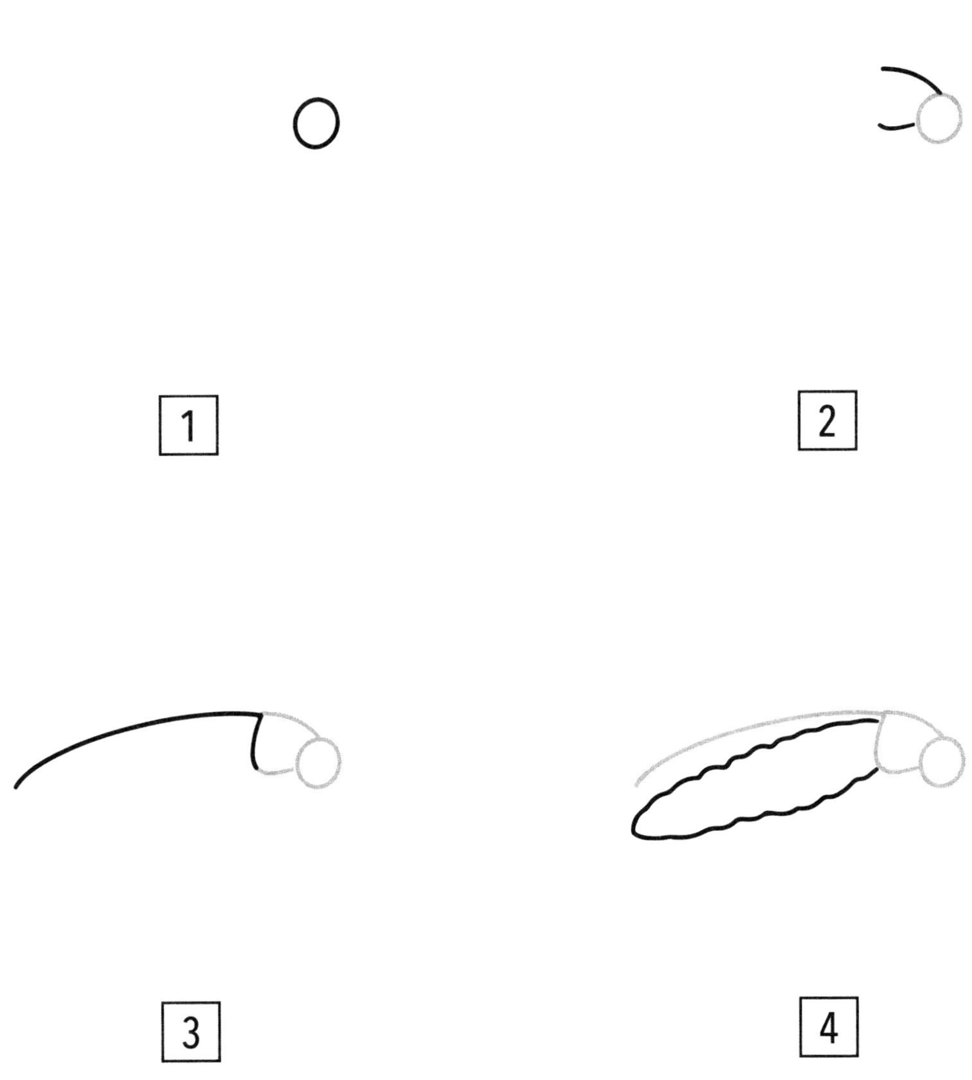

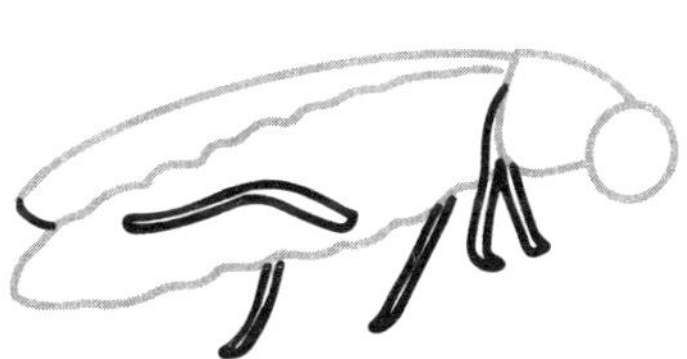

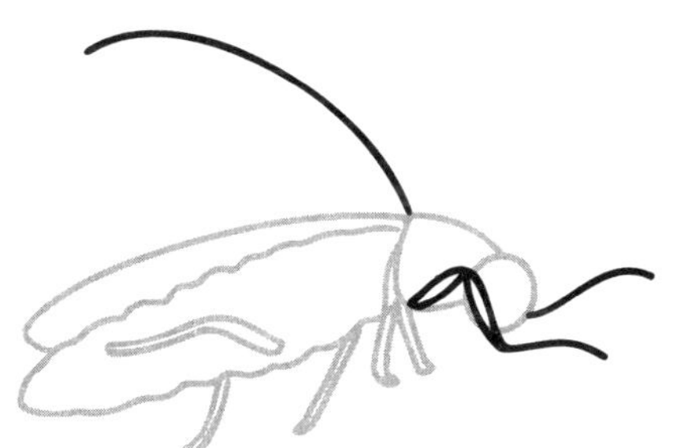

5

6

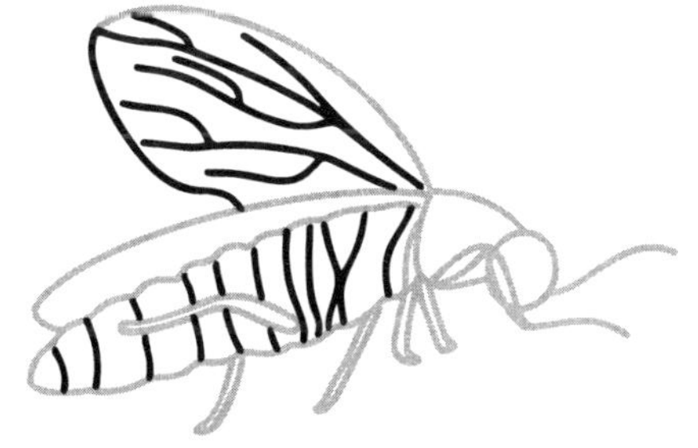

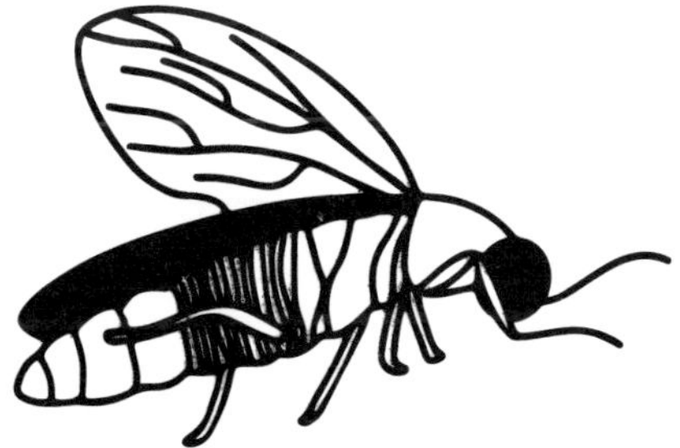

7

8

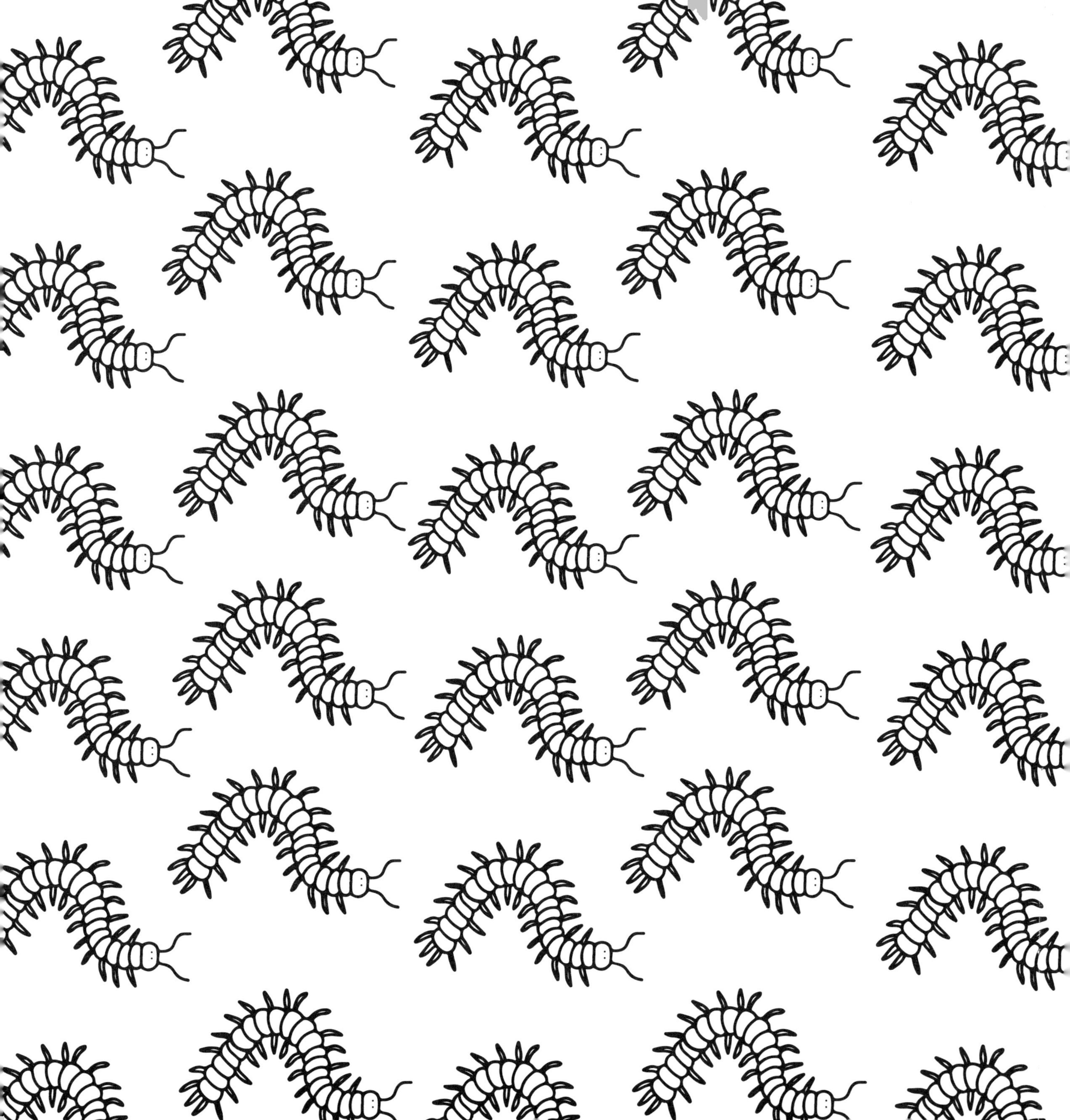

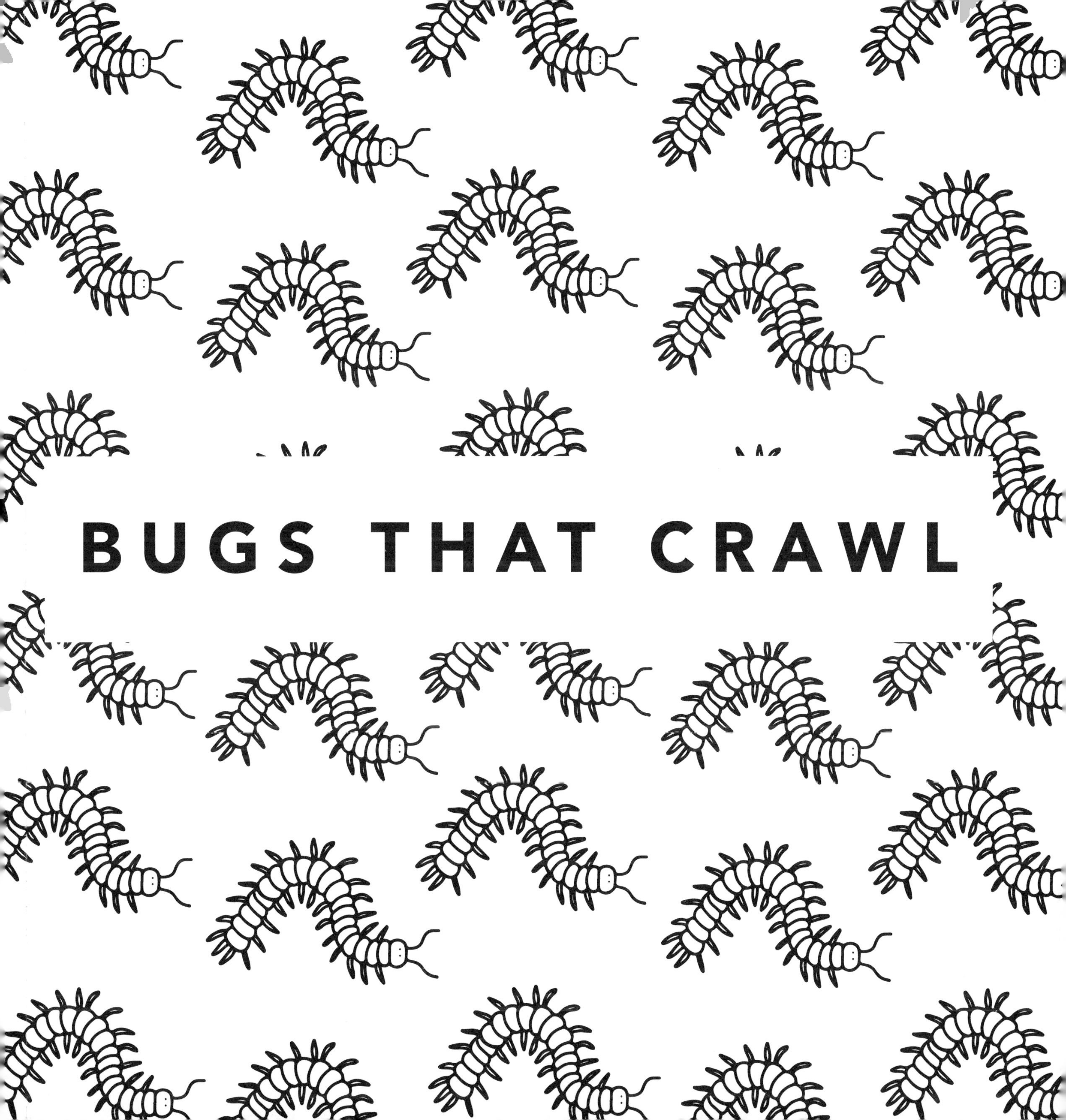

BUGS THAT CRAWL

CYCLOMMATUS BEETLE

Cyclommatus beetles gleam in colors of gold, copper, and emerald green, their metallic shells changing with every shift of light.

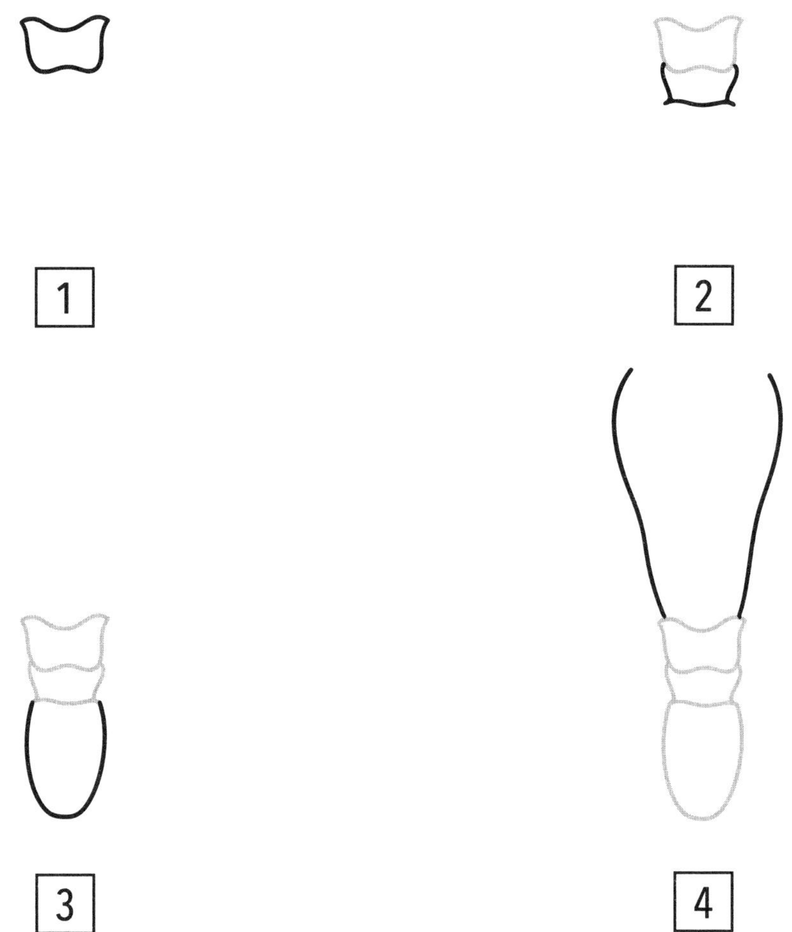

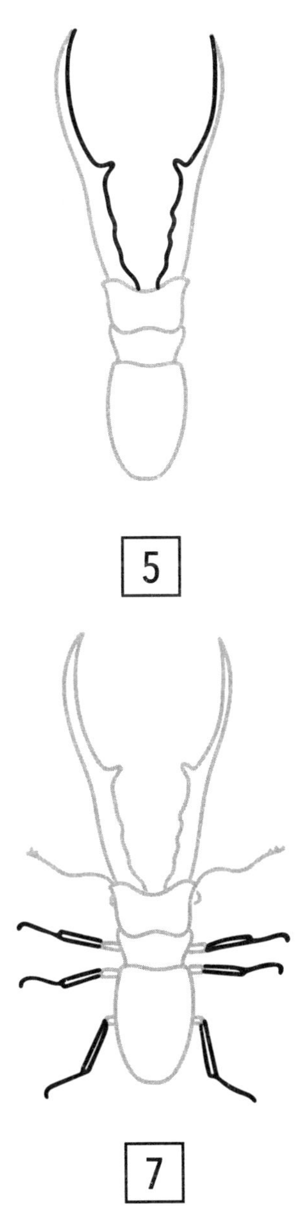

5

6

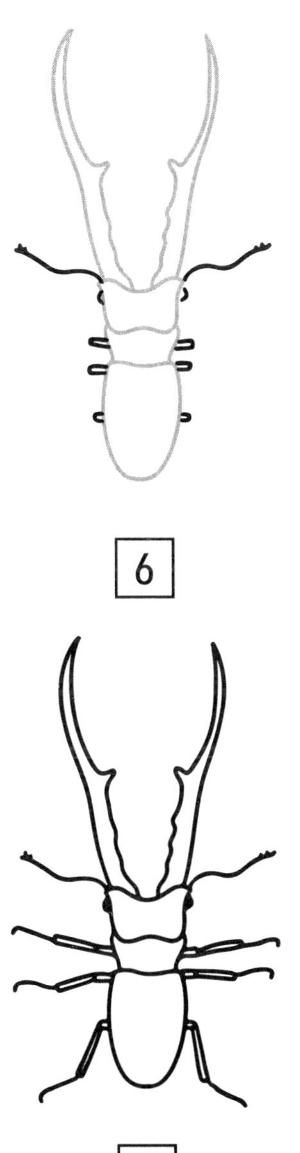

7

8

RAINBOW SCARAB BEETLE

Despite being a dung beetle that rolls animal poop into balls, the rainbow scarab beetle is one of the shiniest beetles on Earth.

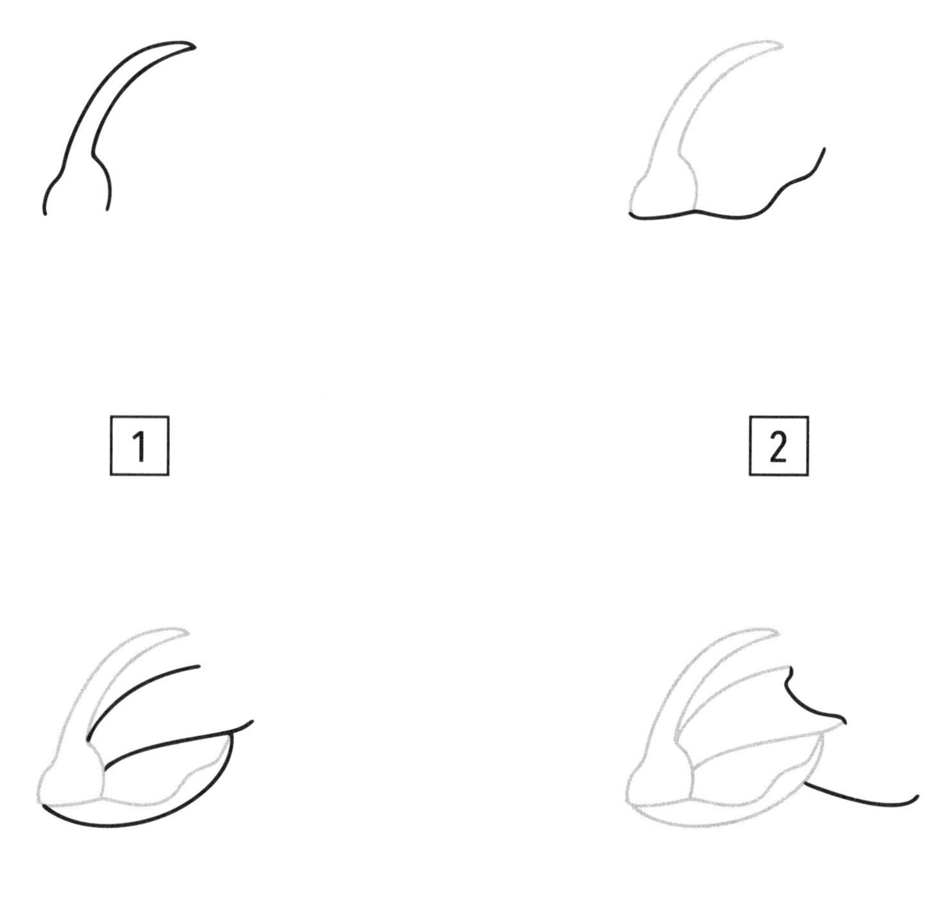

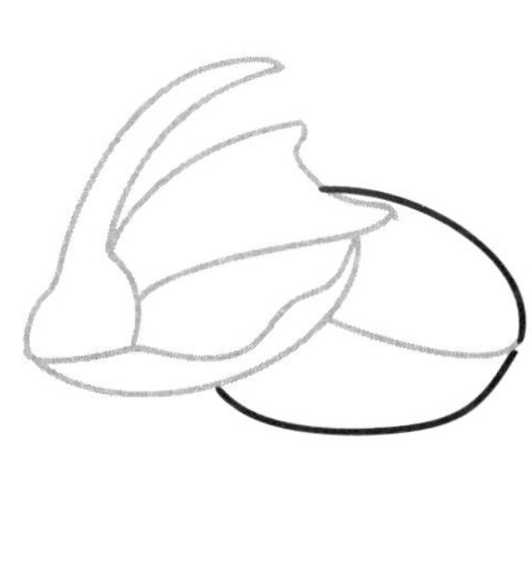

5

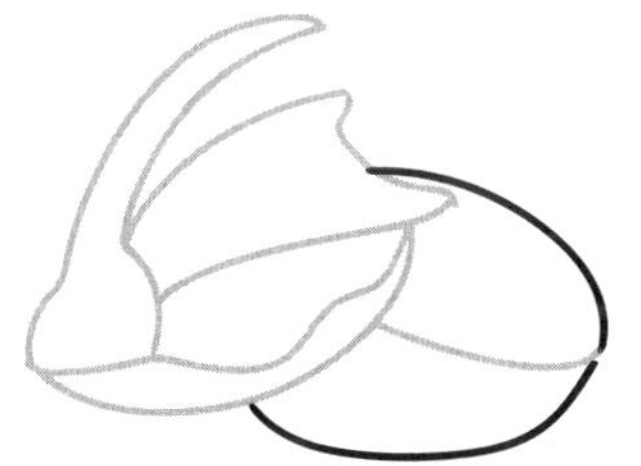

6

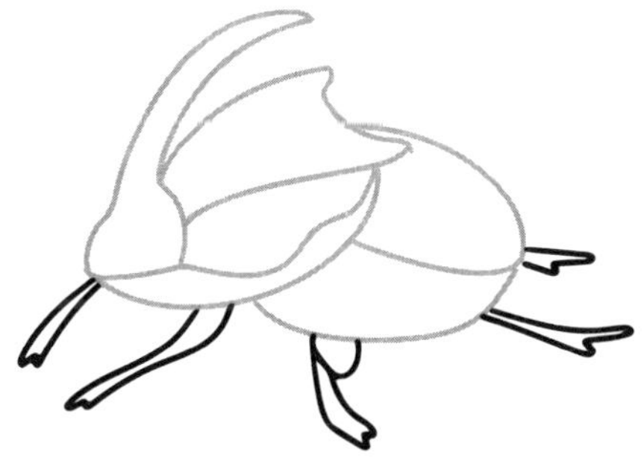

7

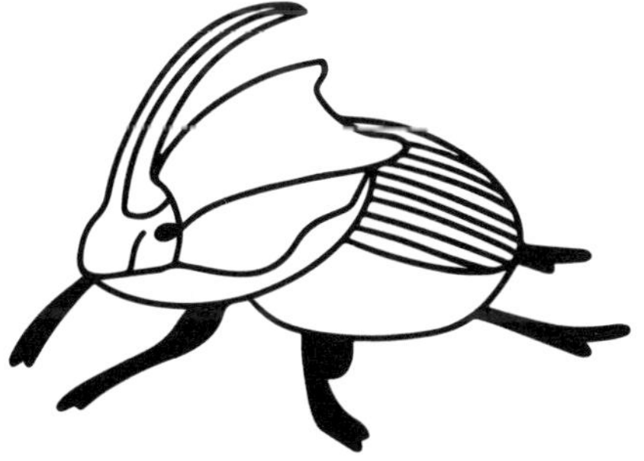

8

DADDY LONGLEGS

Daddy longlegs aren't true spiders. They're called *harvestmen*, and they don't spin webs or have venom. They just wander around on super-long legs!

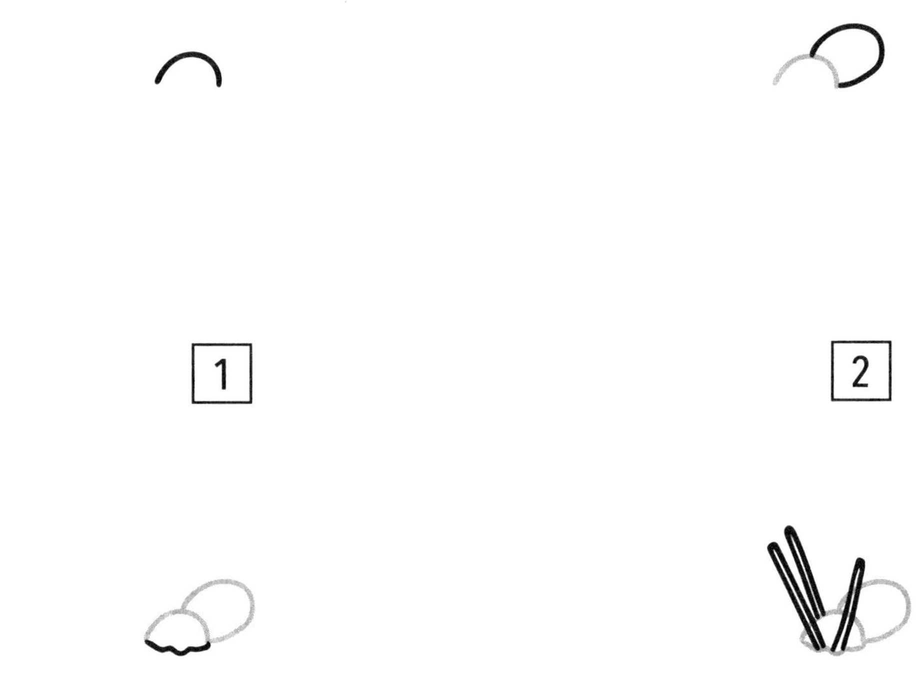

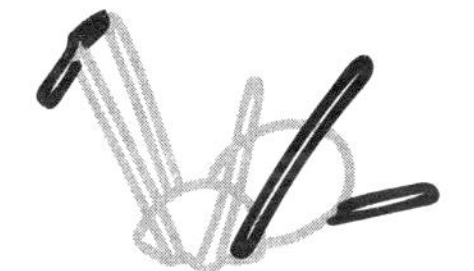

5

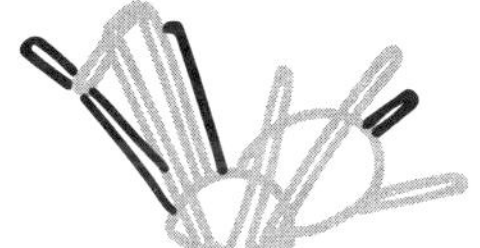

6

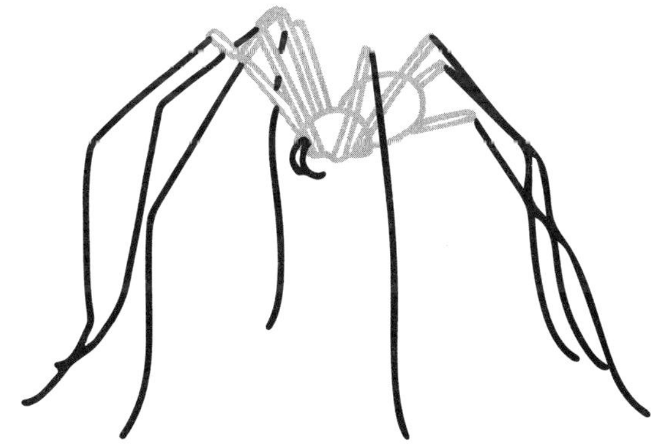

7

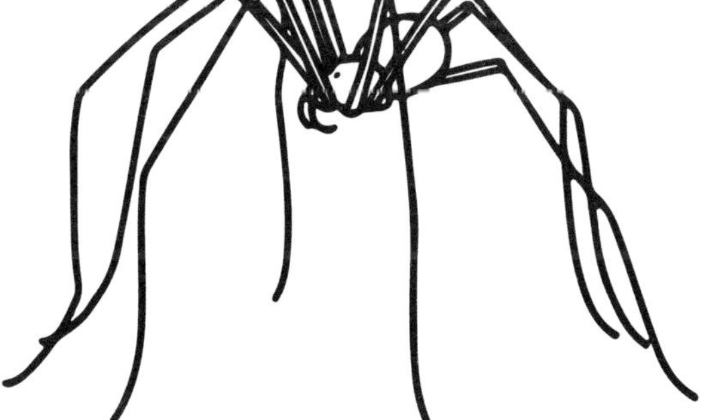

8

WOOLLY WORM CATERPILLAR

Legend says you can predict winter by looking at a woolly worm's stripes. More black means a harsher winter and more orange means a milder winter is in store.

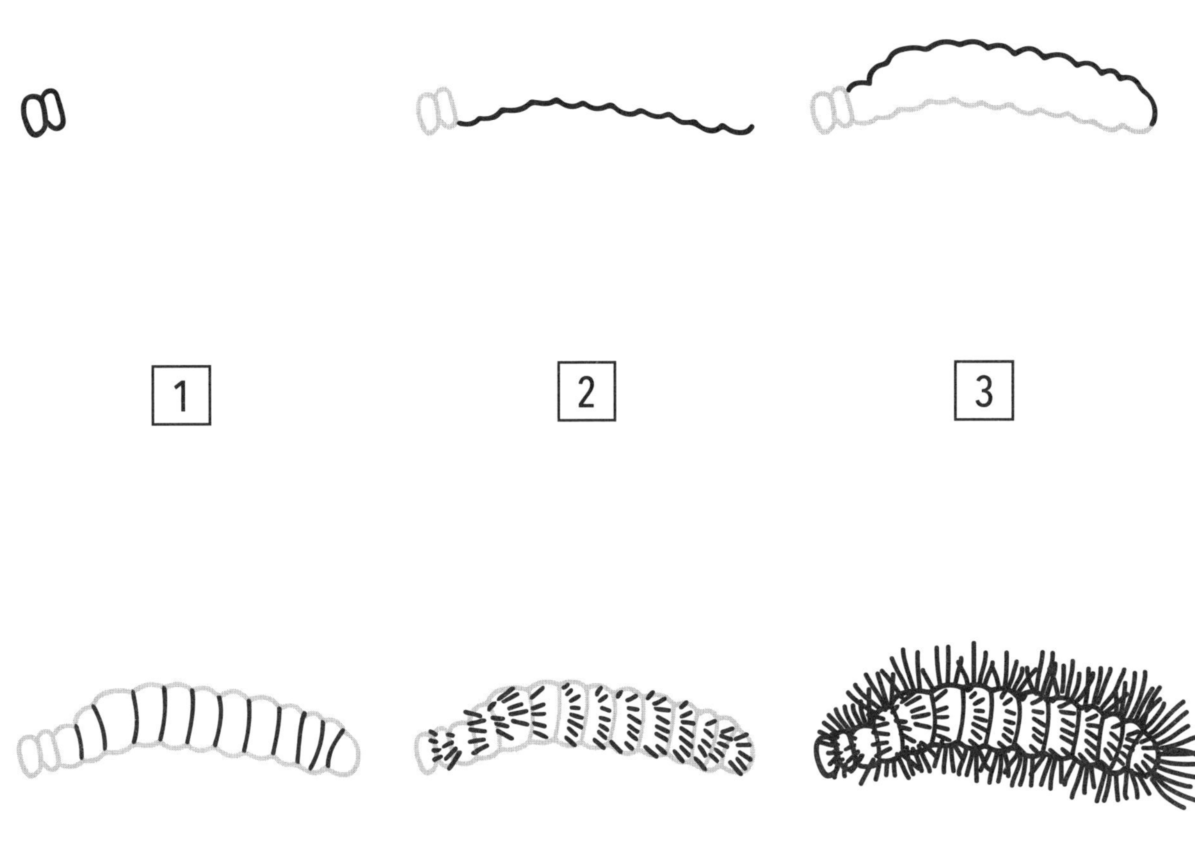

CENTIPEDE

Despite their name, centipedes can have anywhere from 30 to over 350 legs. They're fast, venomous predators that use their front legs as fangs to hunt insects, spiders, and even small amphibians.

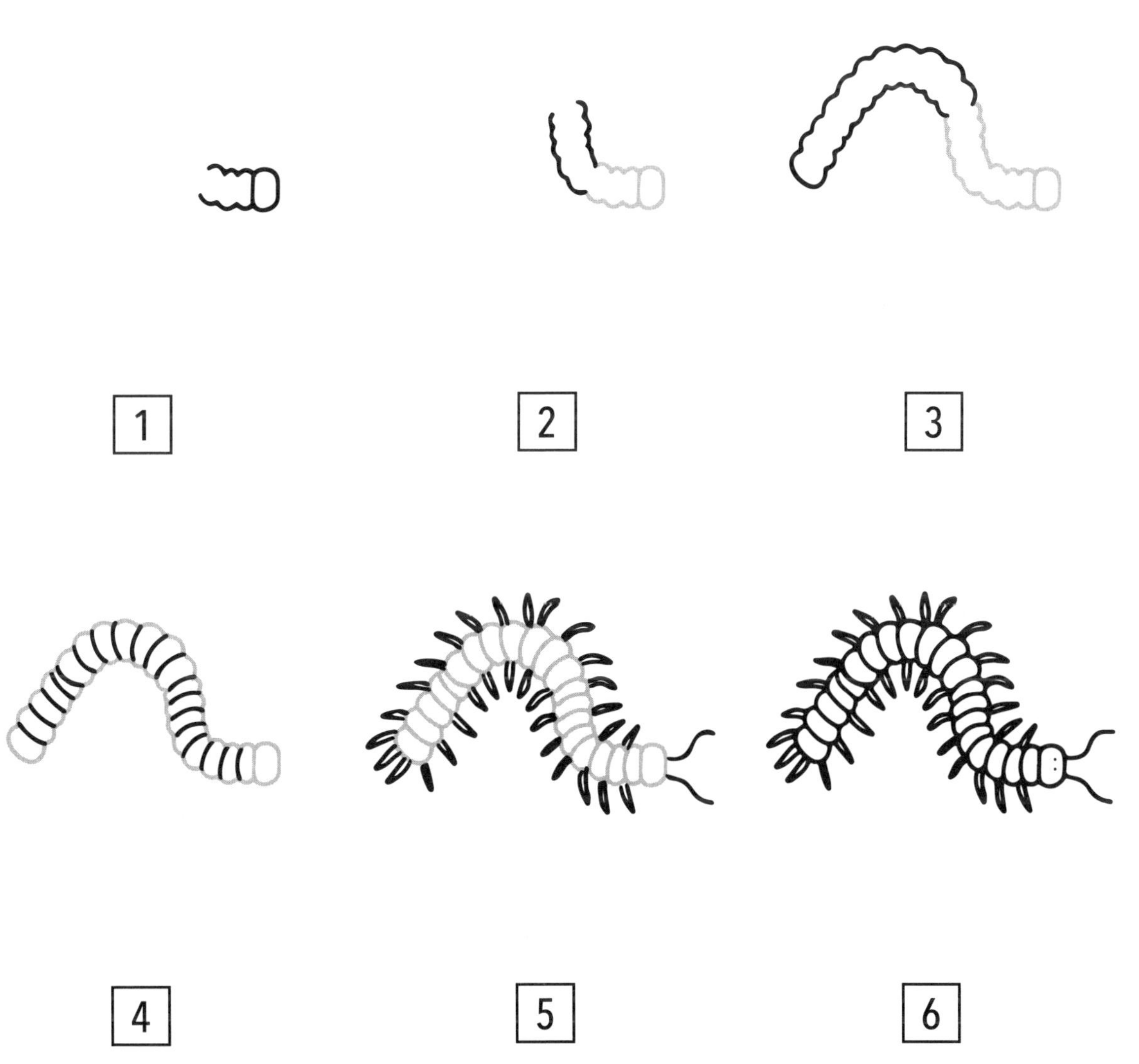

LEAF INSECT

Leaf insects don't just look like leaves—they sway in the wind to make their camouflage more convincing.

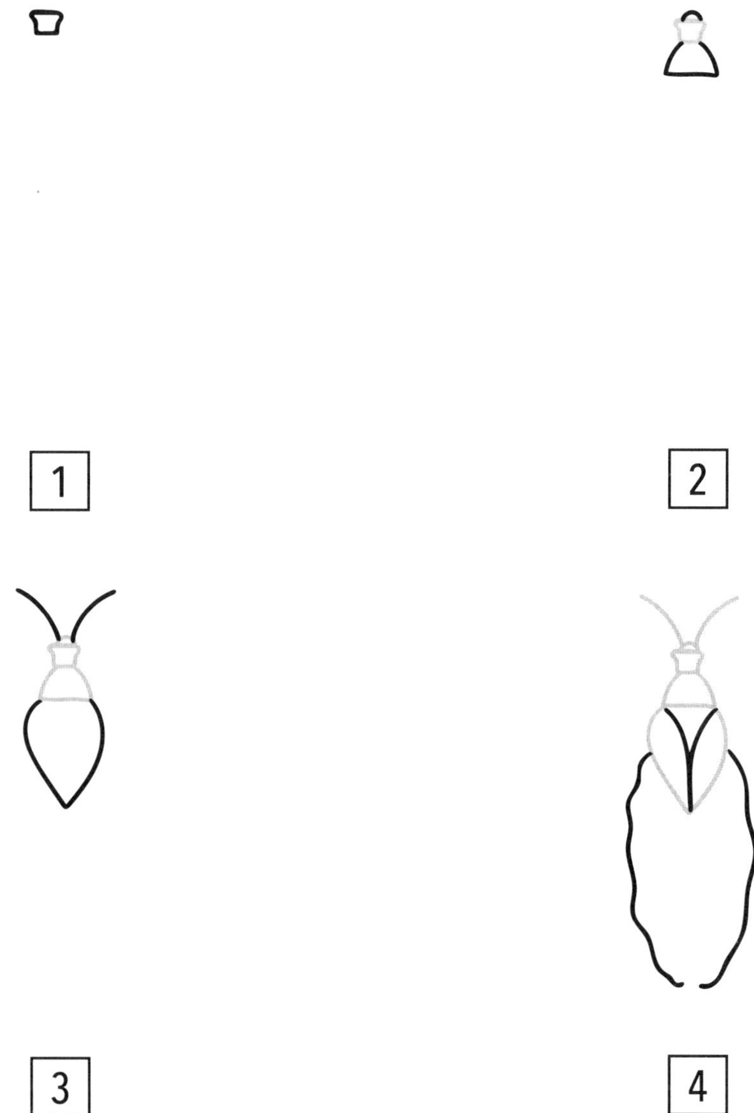

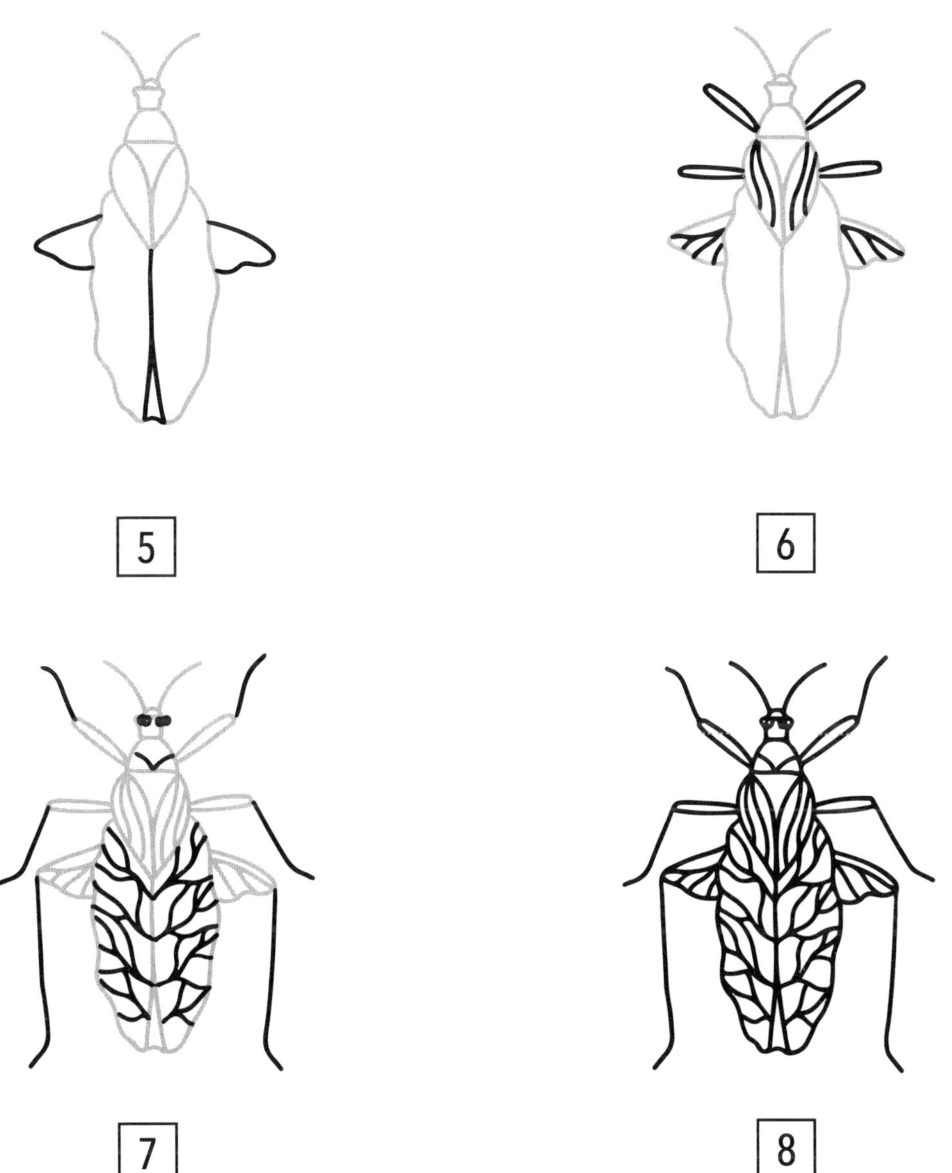

5
6
7
8

TARANTULA

Tarantulas defend themselves from predators by shooting tiny hairs from their bodies that make other animals itch for days.

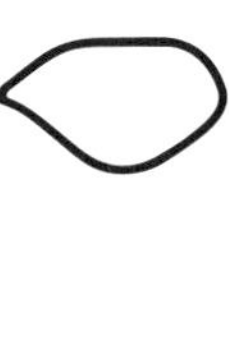

1

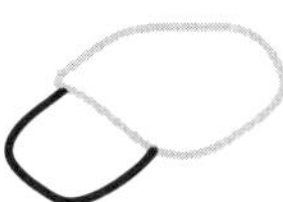

2

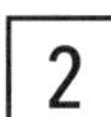

3

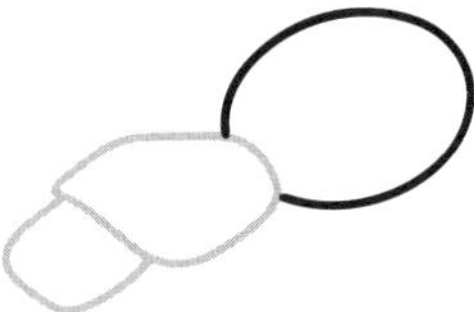

4

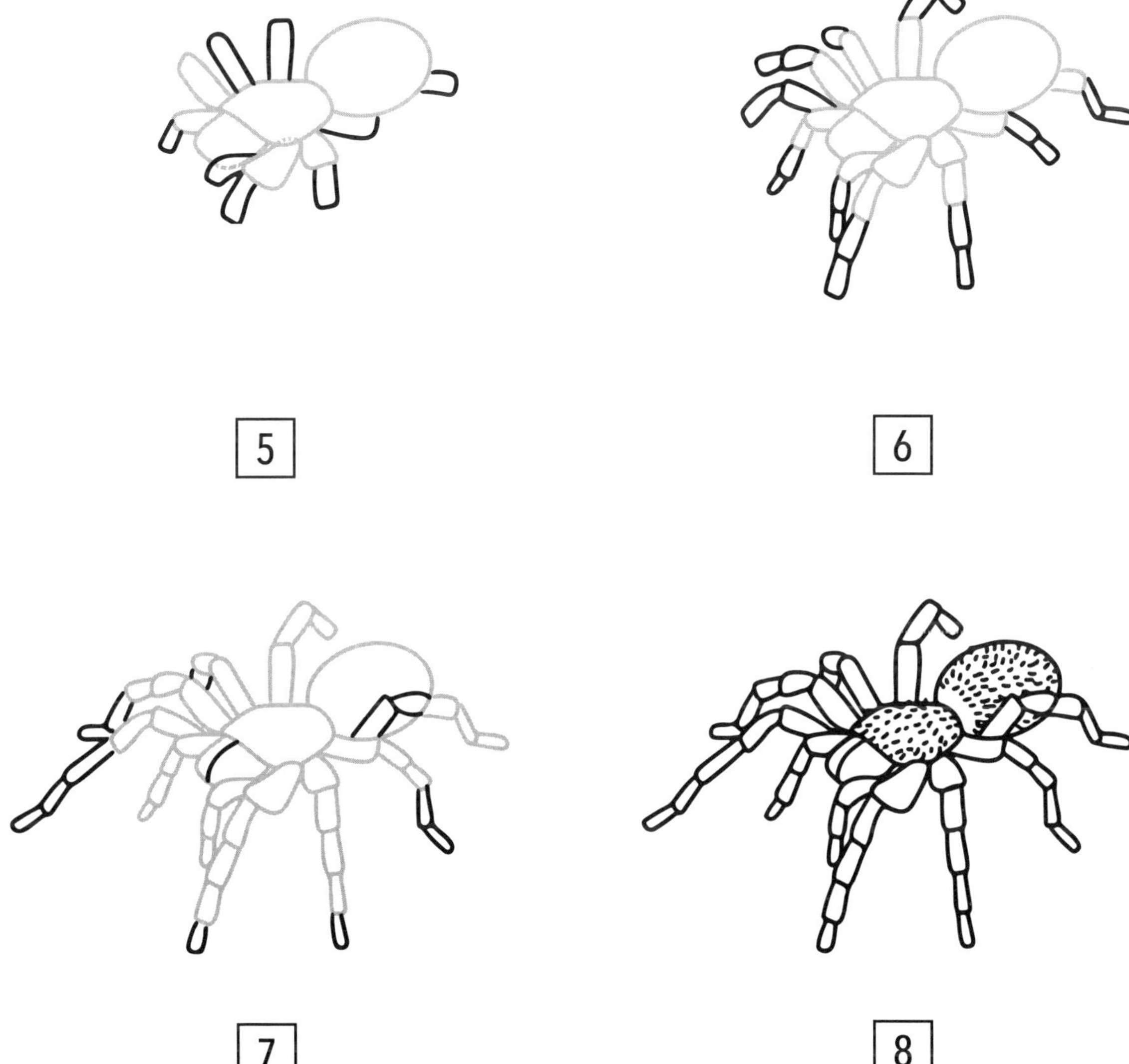

5
6
7
8

KATYDID

Katydids get their name from the sound they make by rubbing their wings together, which sounds like "katy-did, katy-did."

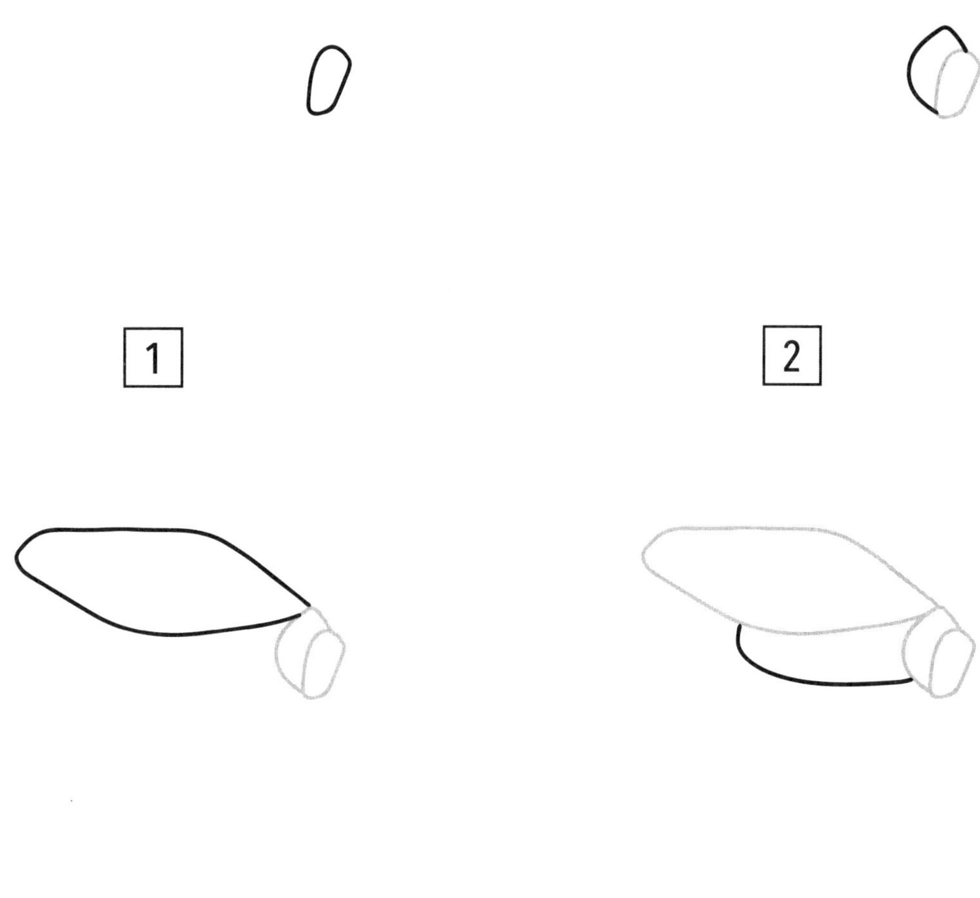

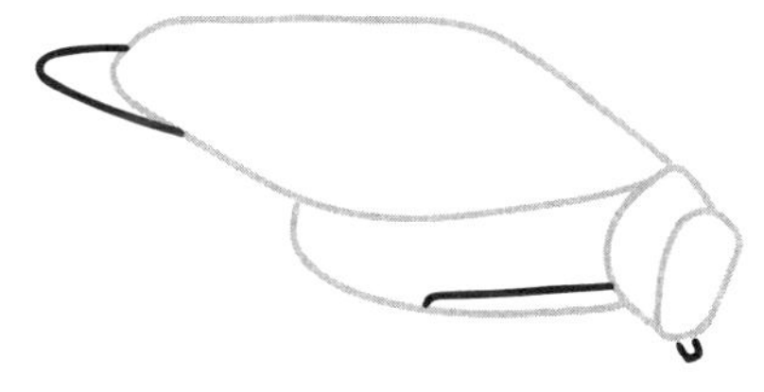

5

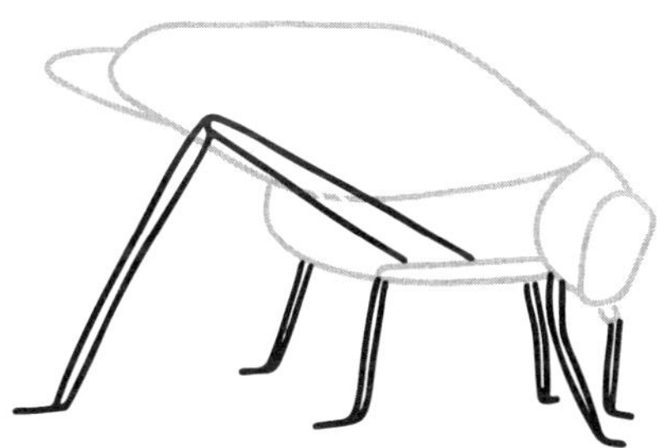

6

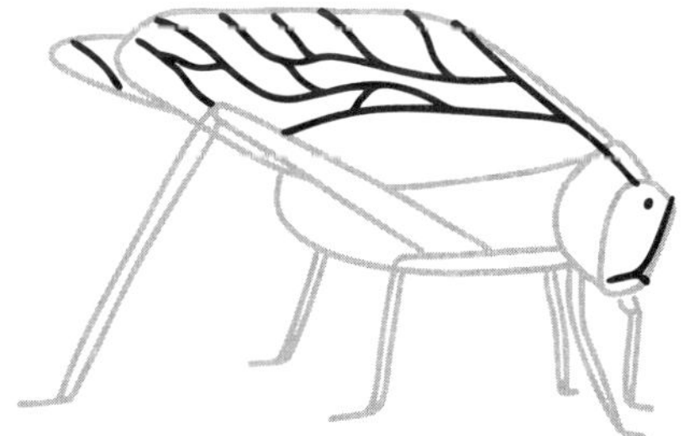

7

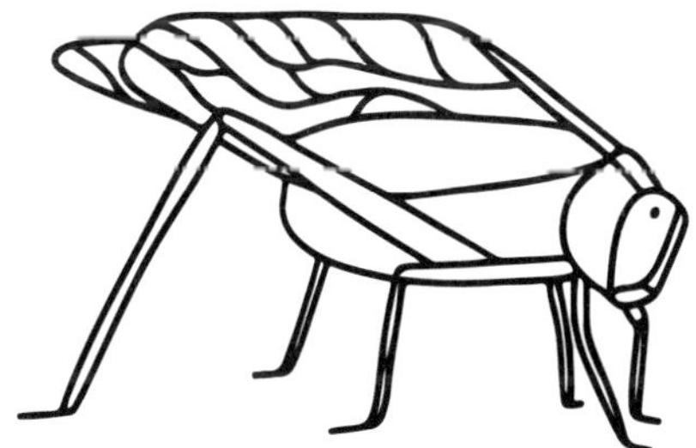

8

PRAYING MANTIS

Praying mantises have triangular heads that can turn nearly 180 degrees, so they can spot dinner sneaking up behind them.

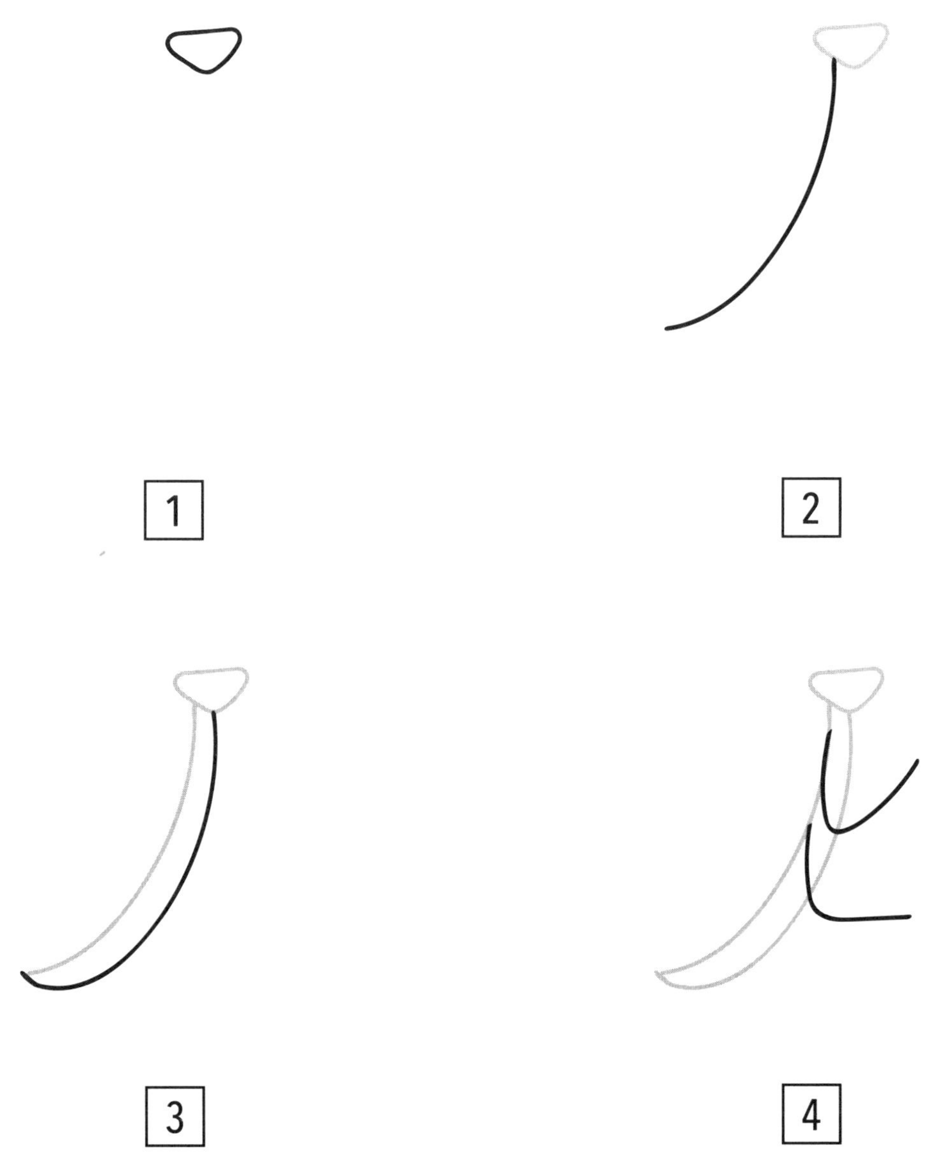

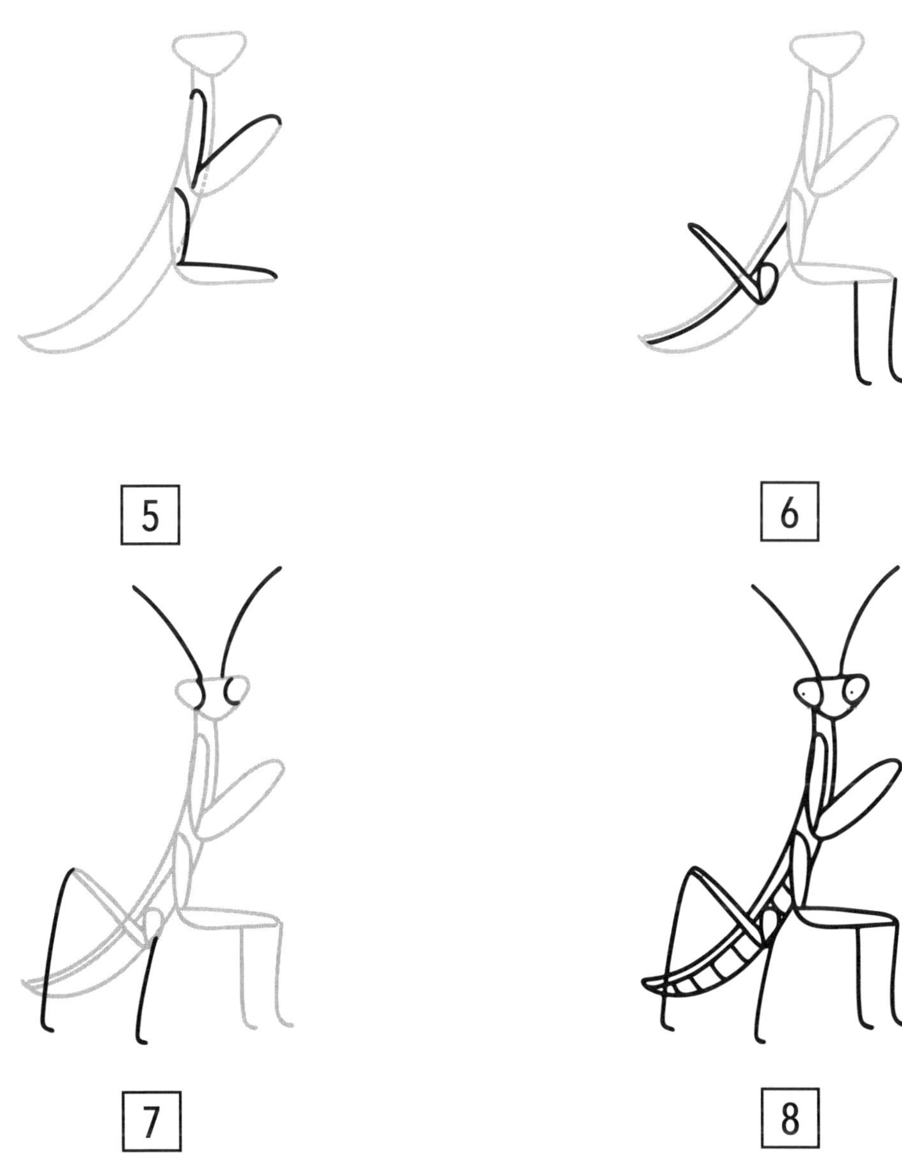

5
6
7
8

ORB WEAVER SPIDER

An orb weaver spider spins a brand-new spiral web each night that can be over two feet wide.

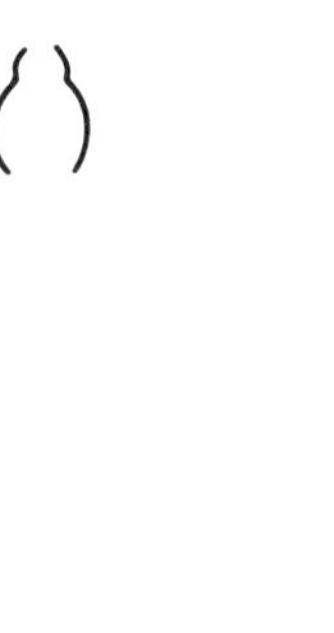

1

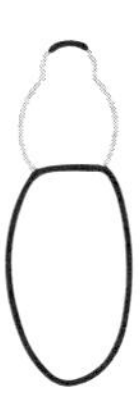

2

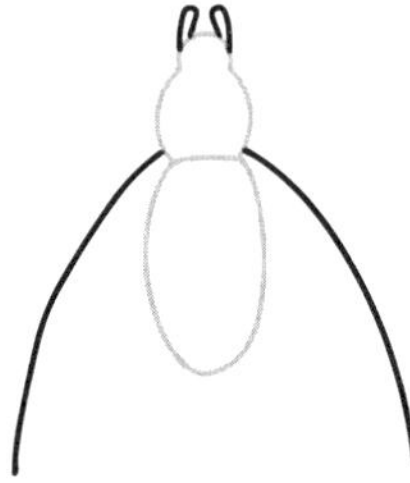

3

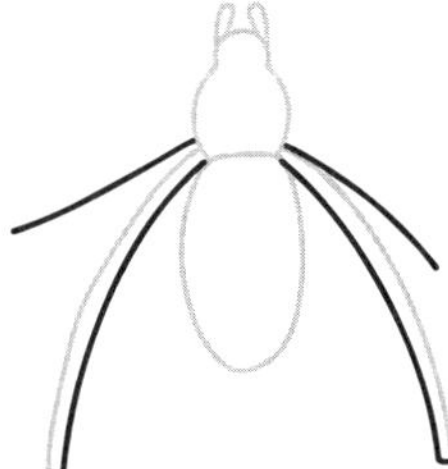

4

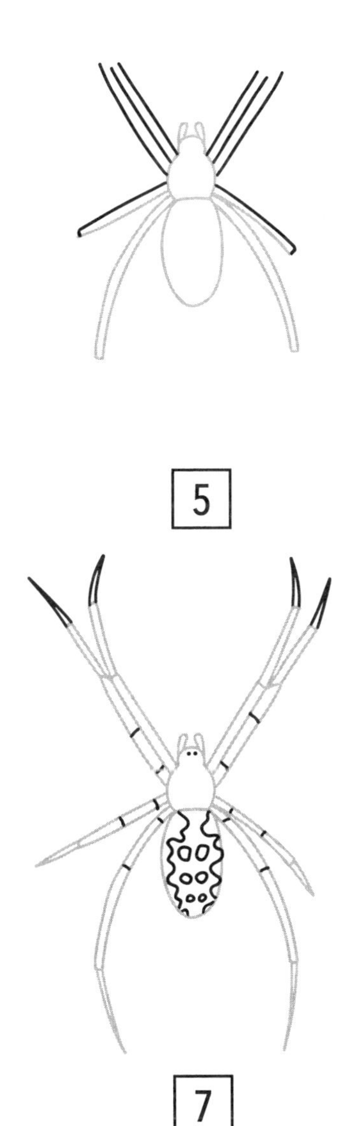

5

6

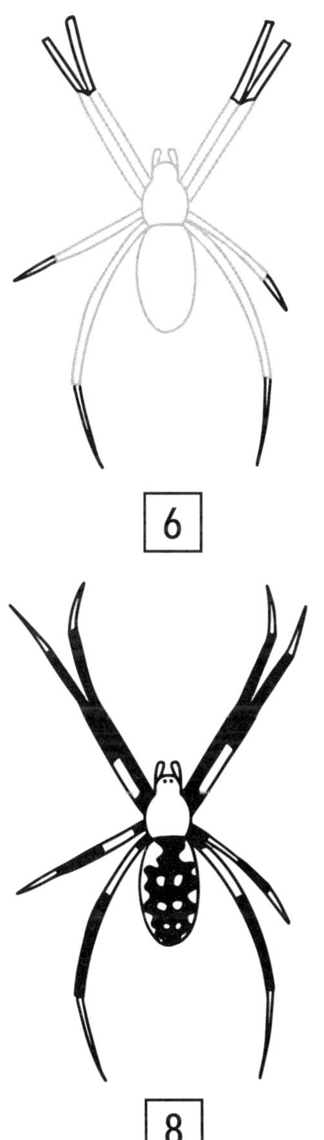

7

8

ANT

Ants live in highly organized colonies with roles like workers, soldiers, and queens and can carry objects up to 50 times their body weight.

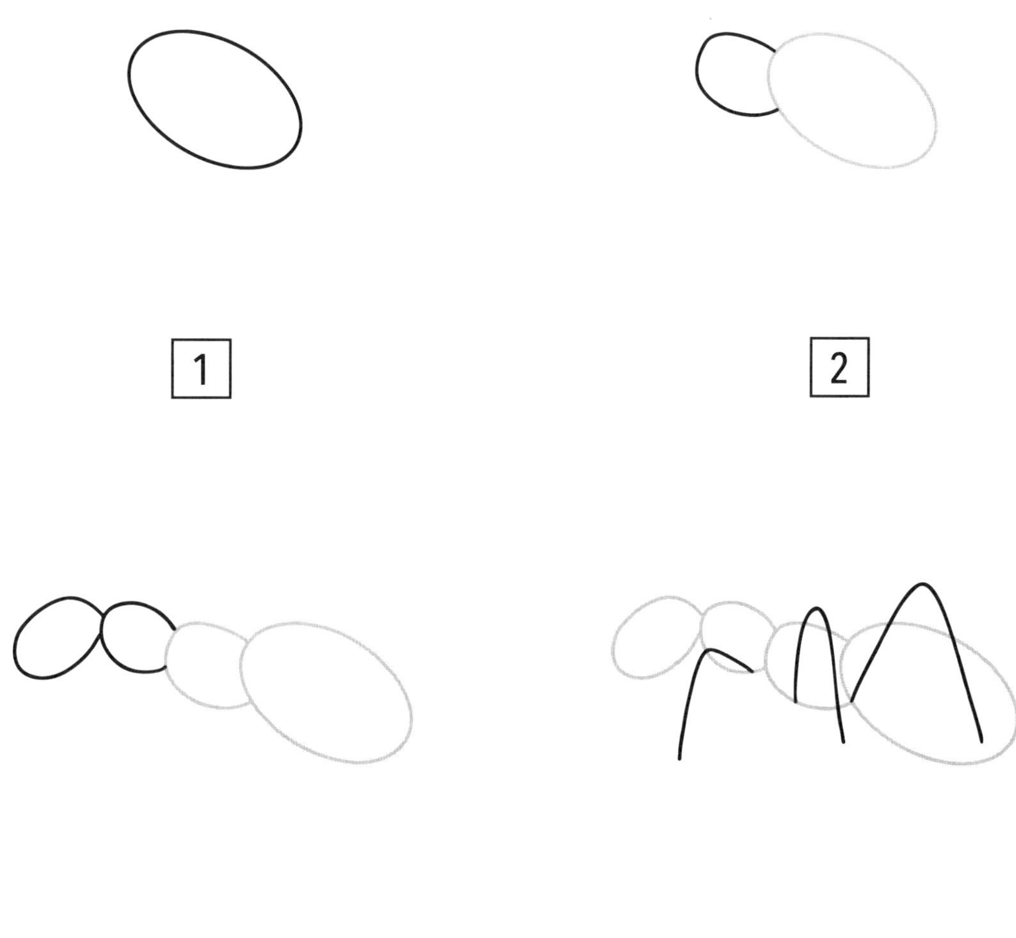

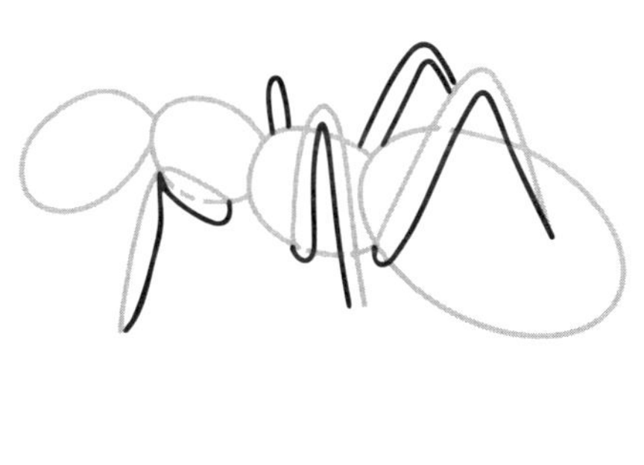

5

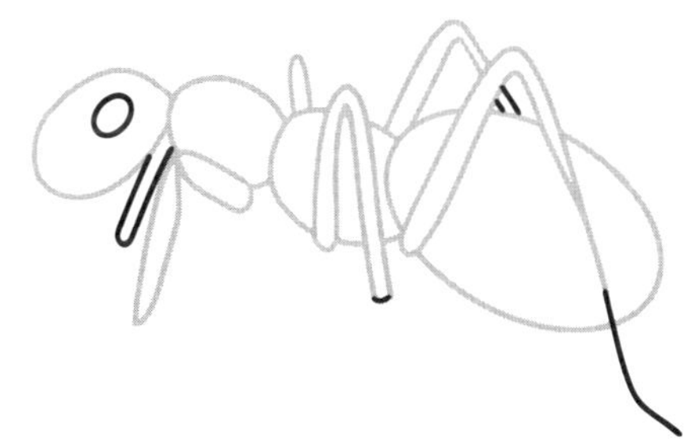

6

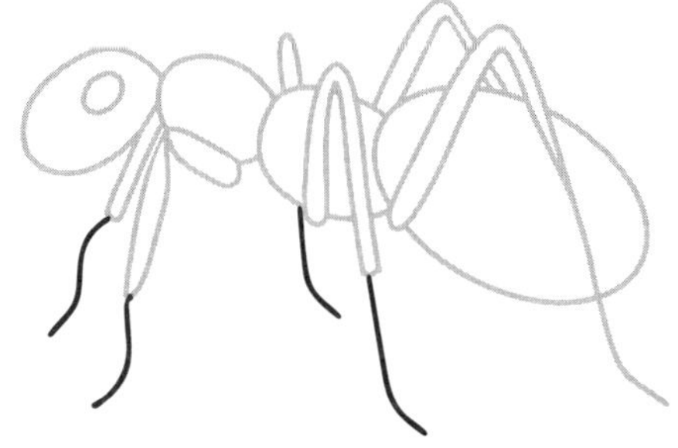

7

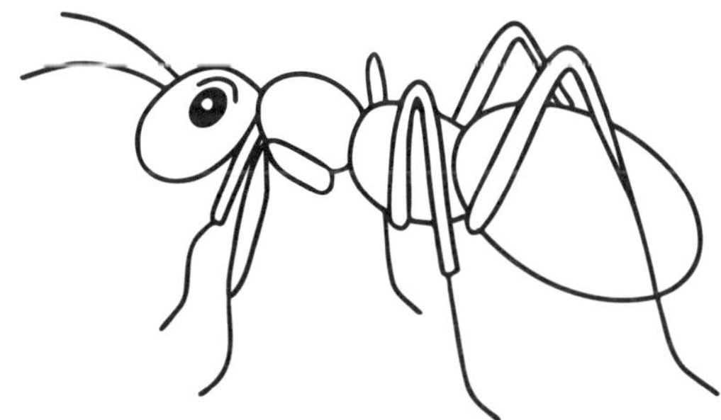

8

JUMPING SPIDER

Jumping spiders have amazing eyesight and can leap up to 50 times their body length to pounce on prey.

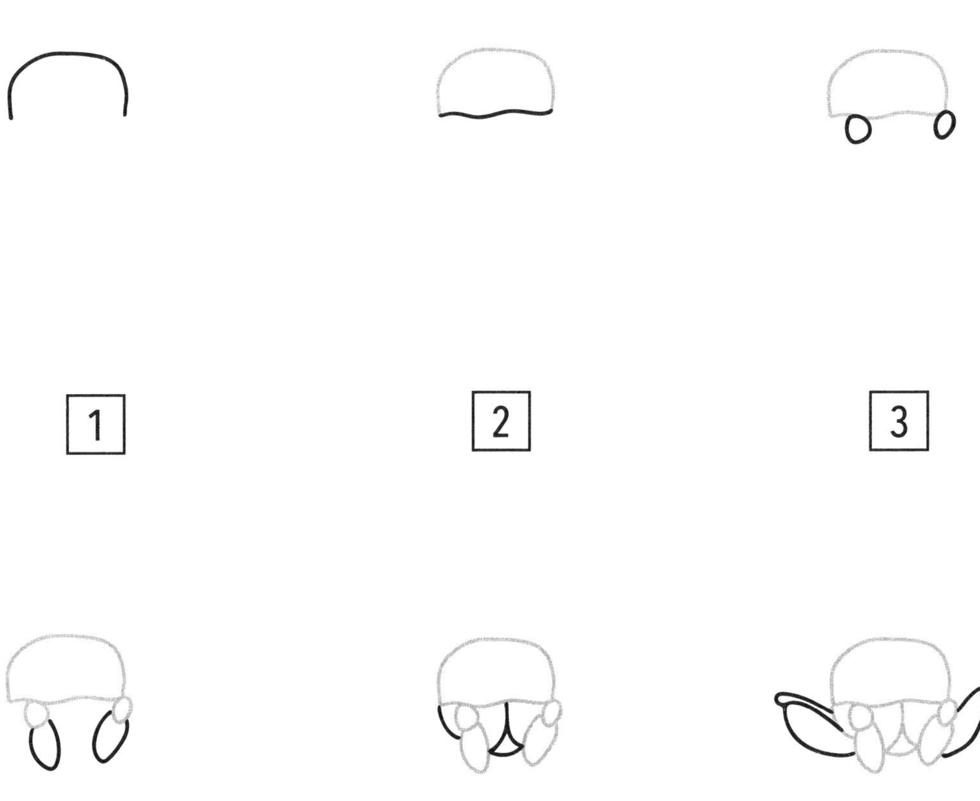

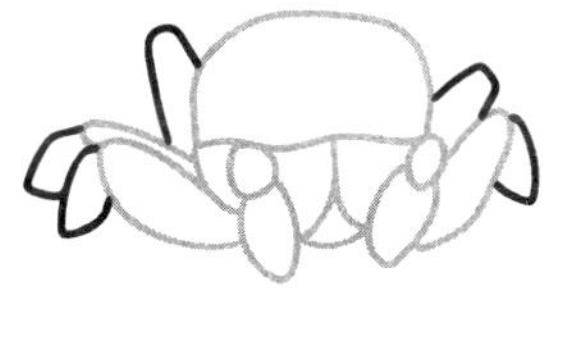

7

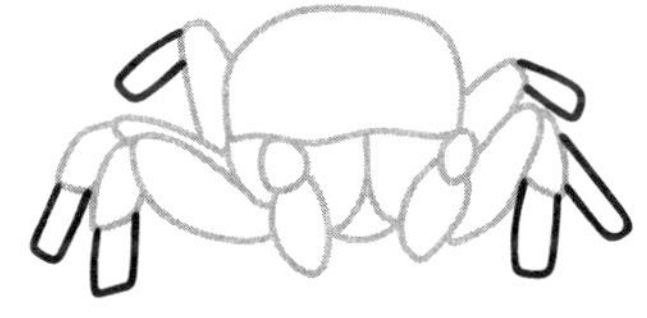

8

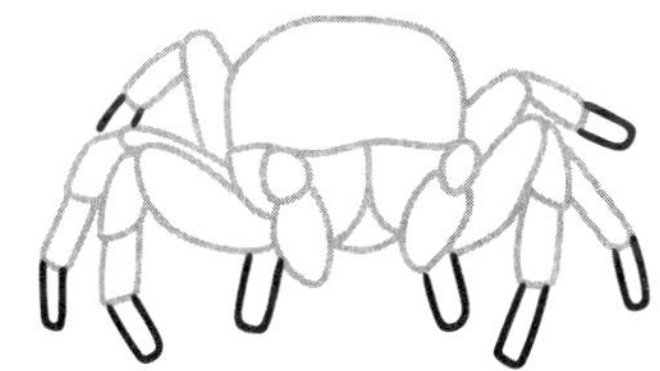

9

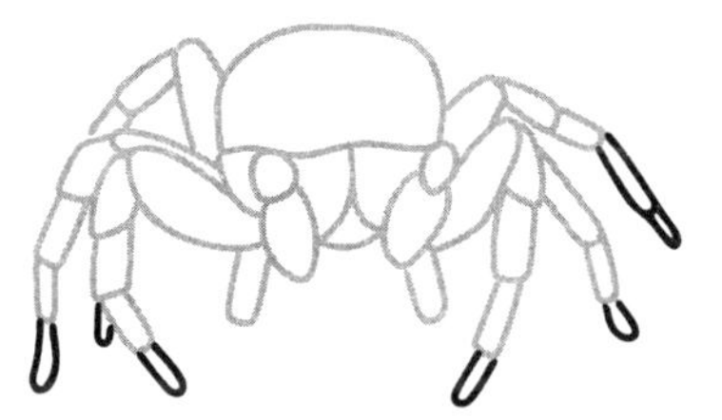

10

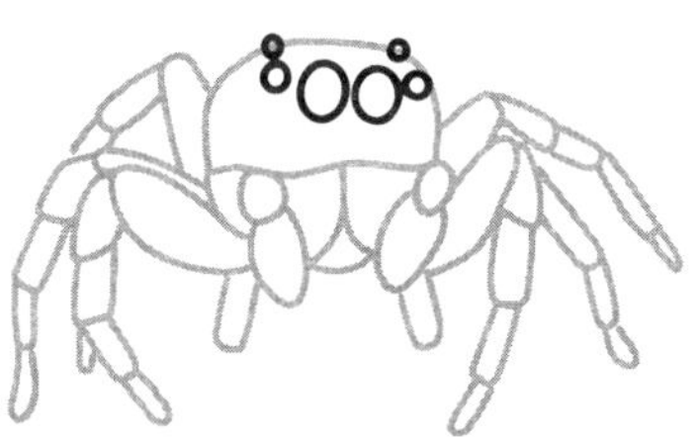

11

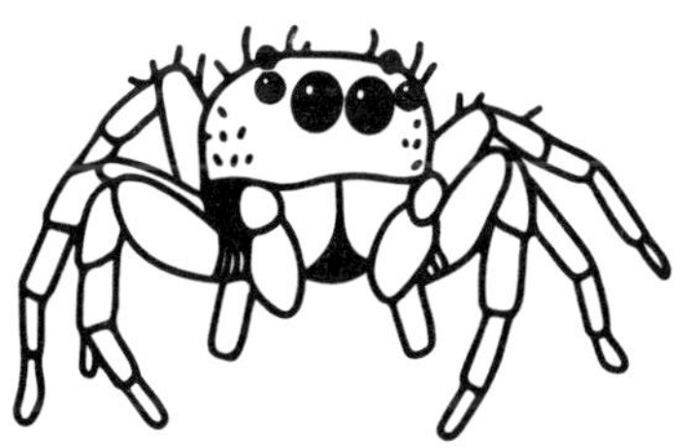

12

ROLY-POLY

Roly-polies aren't insects at all. They're tiny crustaceans, related to shrimp and crabs. They curl into a perfect ball to protect themselves from danger.

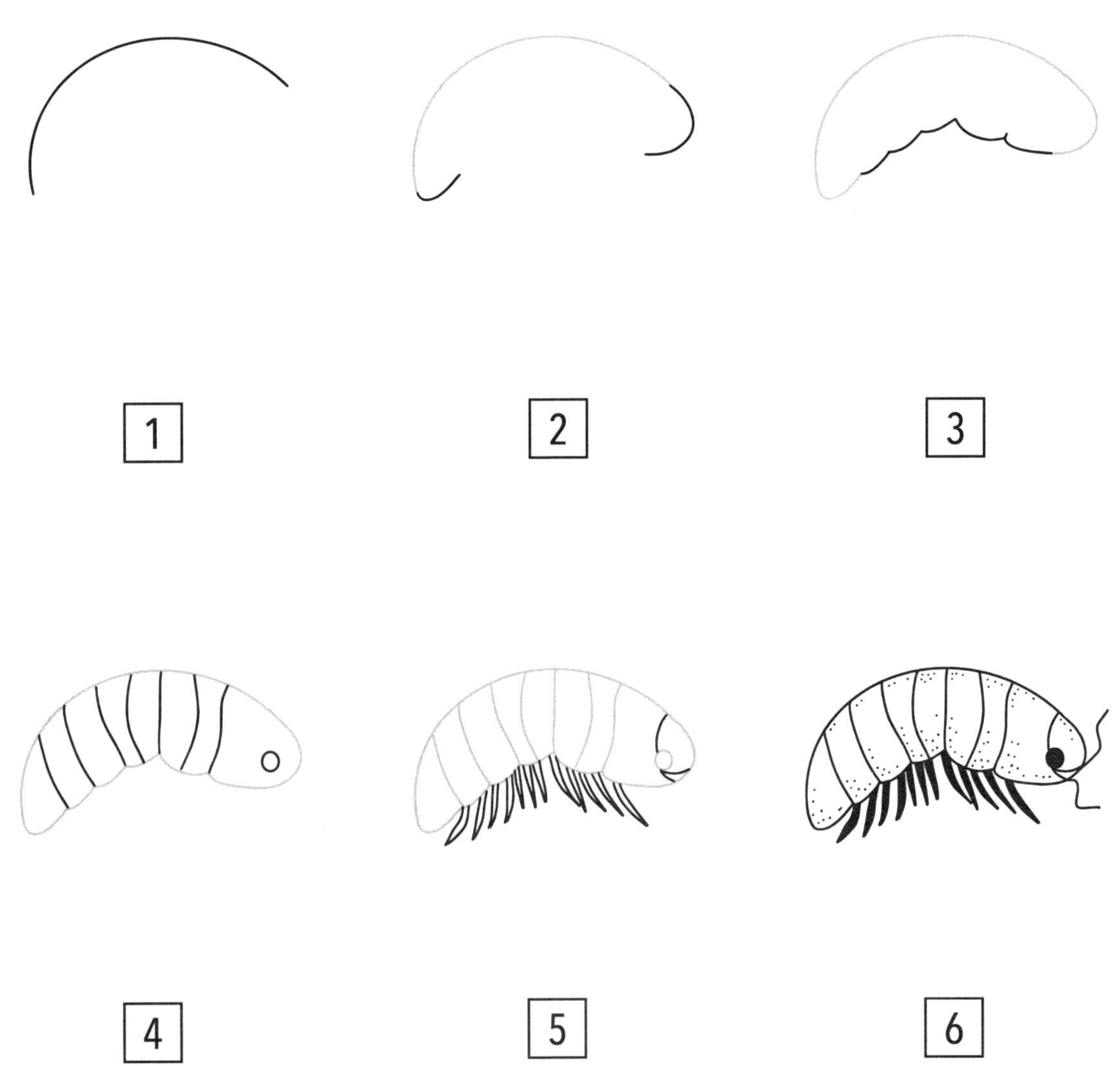

WALKING STICK

Walking sticks are masters of disguise that can stay so still that even birds mistake them for real twigs.

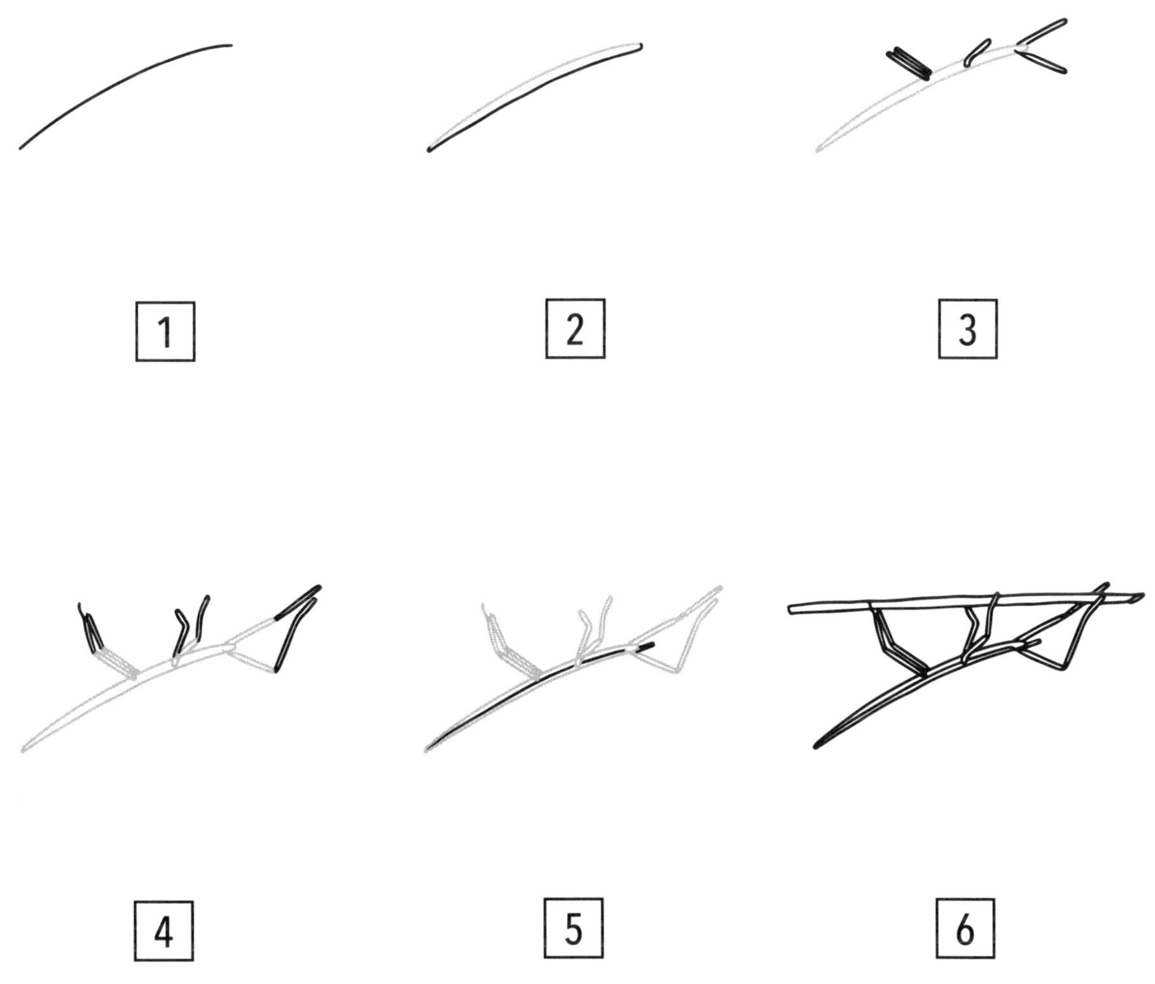

GRASSHOPPER

A grasshopper's legs work like spring-loaded catapults, launching them more than 20 times their body length in a single leap.

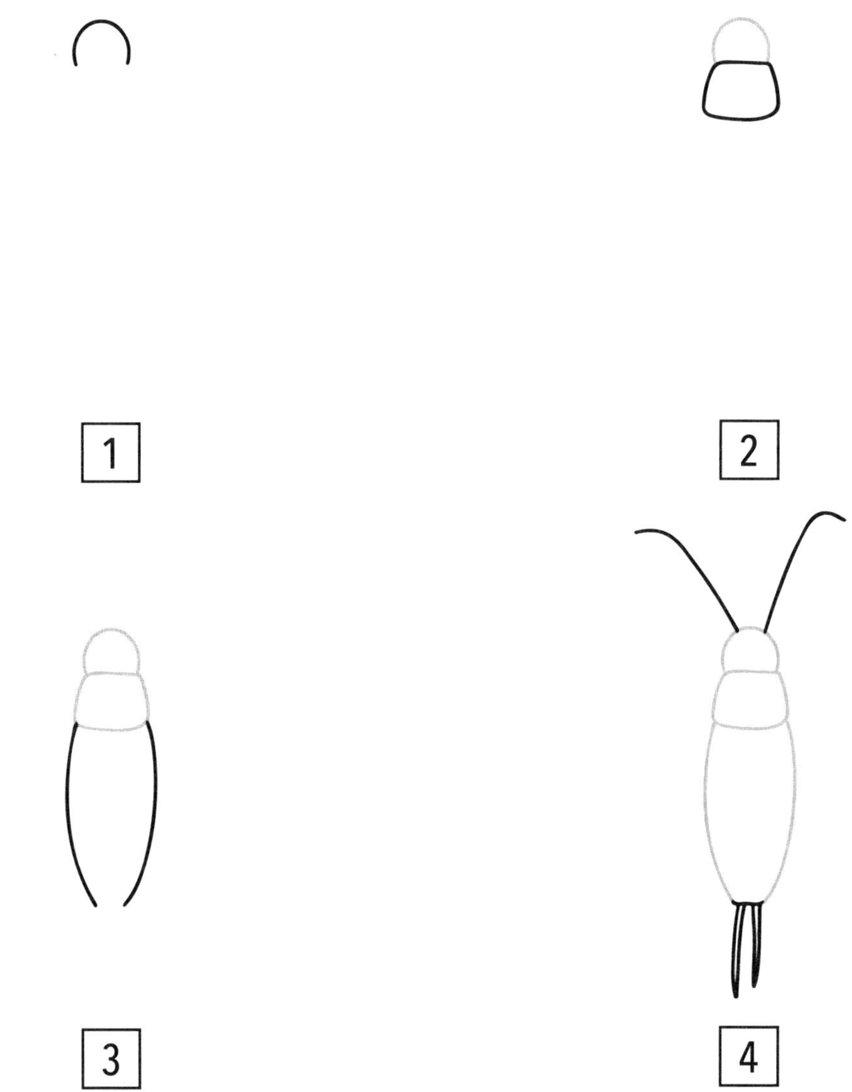

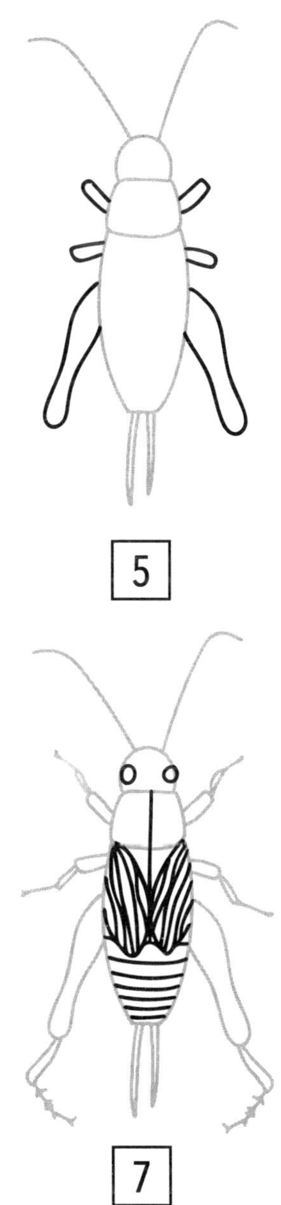

5

6

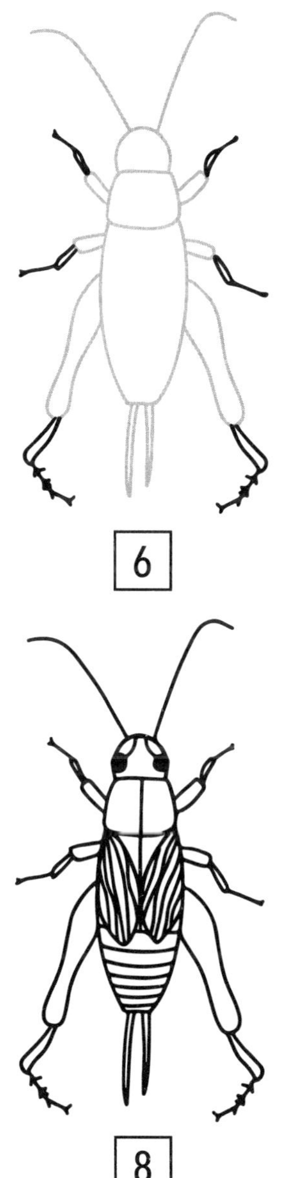

7

8

CRICKET

Only male crickets chirp, and they do it by rubbing their wings together, like playing a tiny violin.

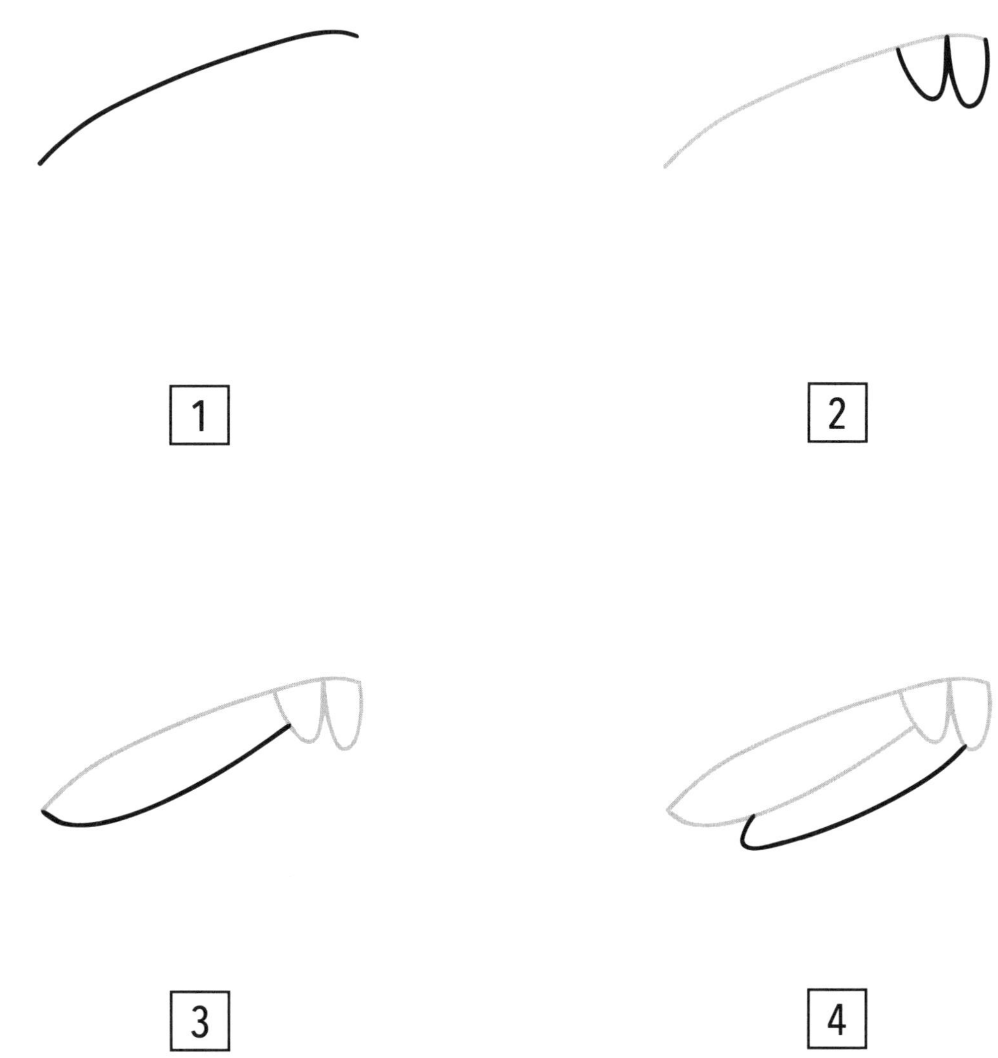

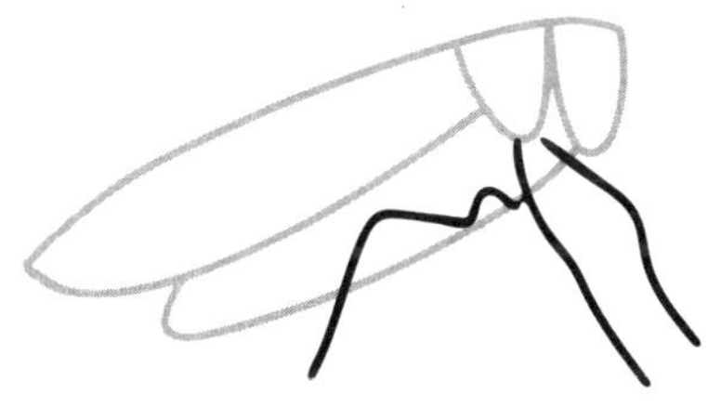

5

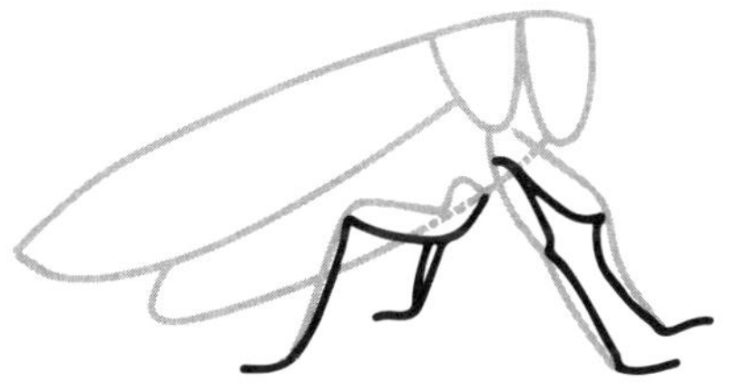

6

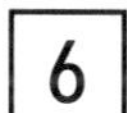

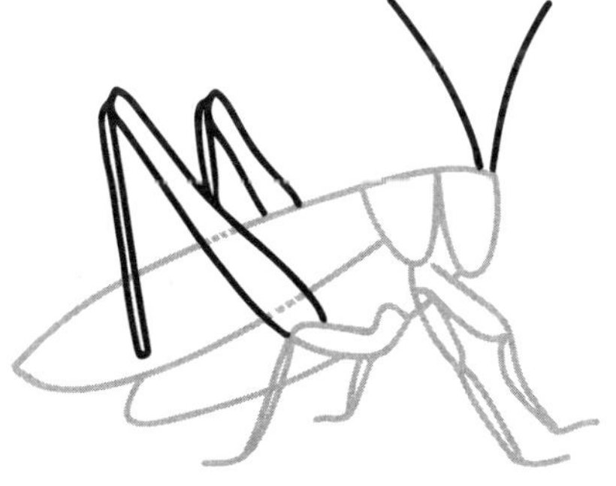

7

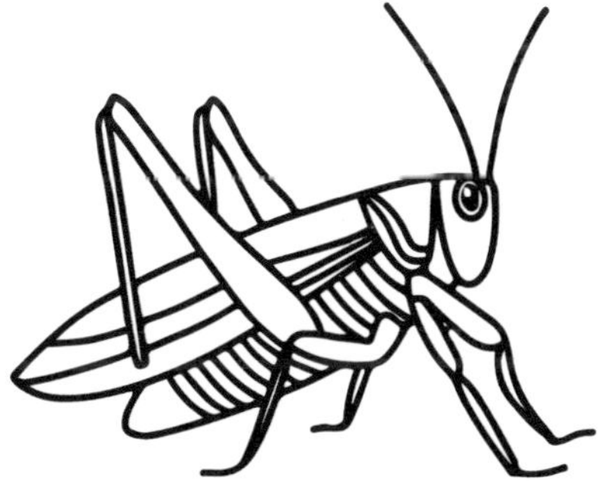

8

WOLF SPIDER

Wolf spiders don't spin webs. Instead, they run after their food using sharp eyes and quick legs. The mother spider carries her eggs, and later her baby spiders, on her back.

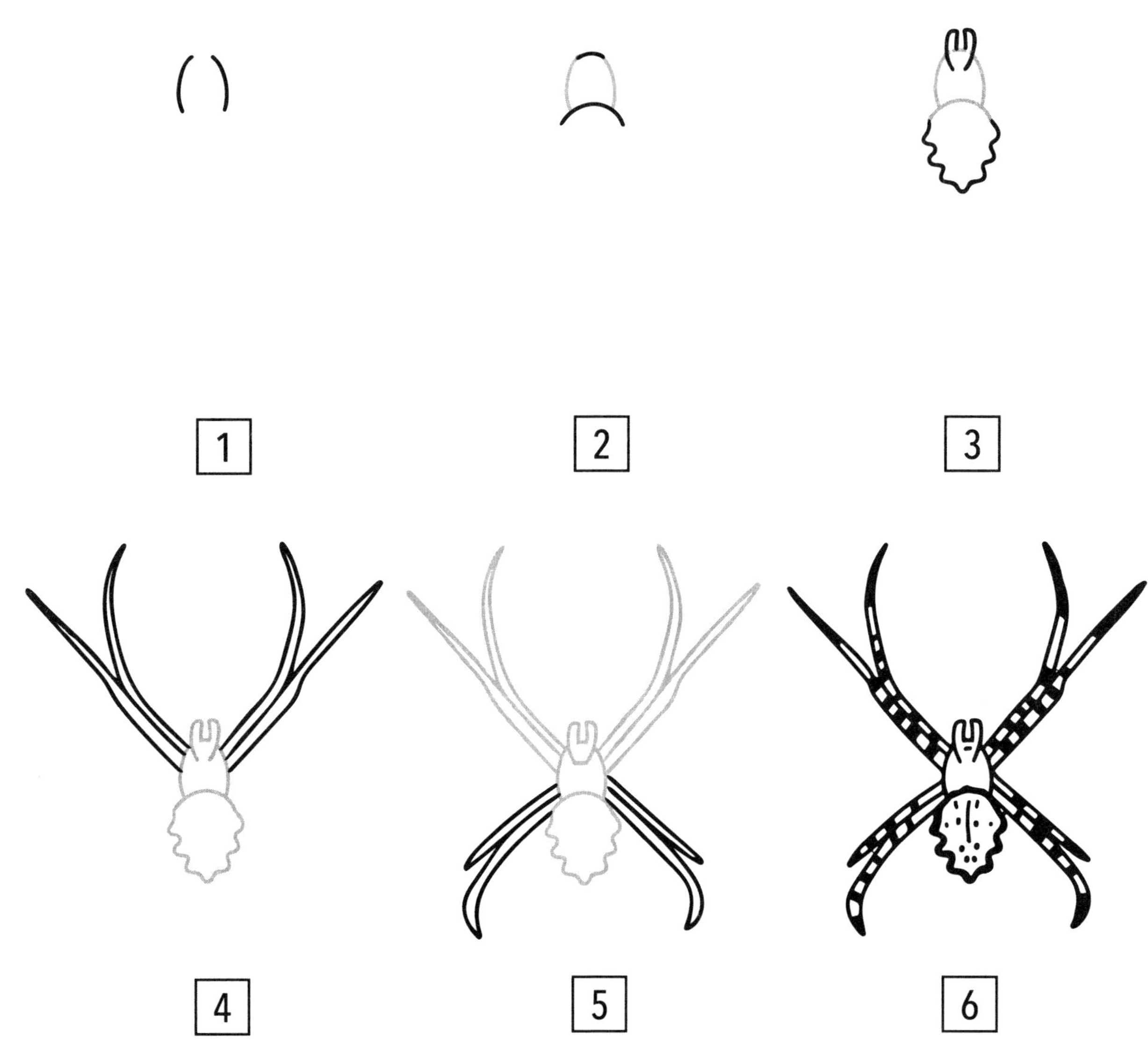

HICKORY HORNED DEVIL CATERPILLAR

This giant green caterpillar can grow as long as a hot dog but its scary-looking horns are actually totally harmless.

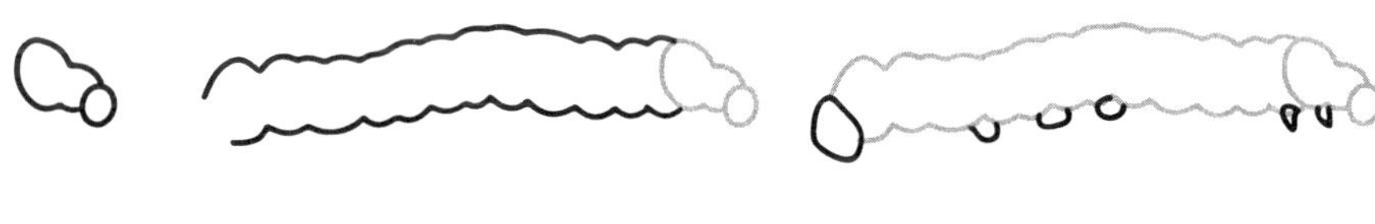

1   2   3

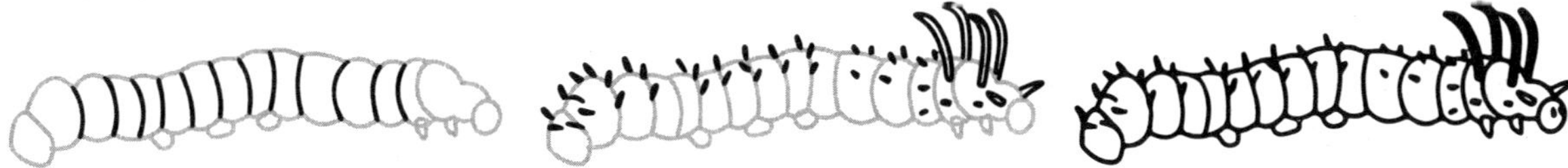

4   5   6

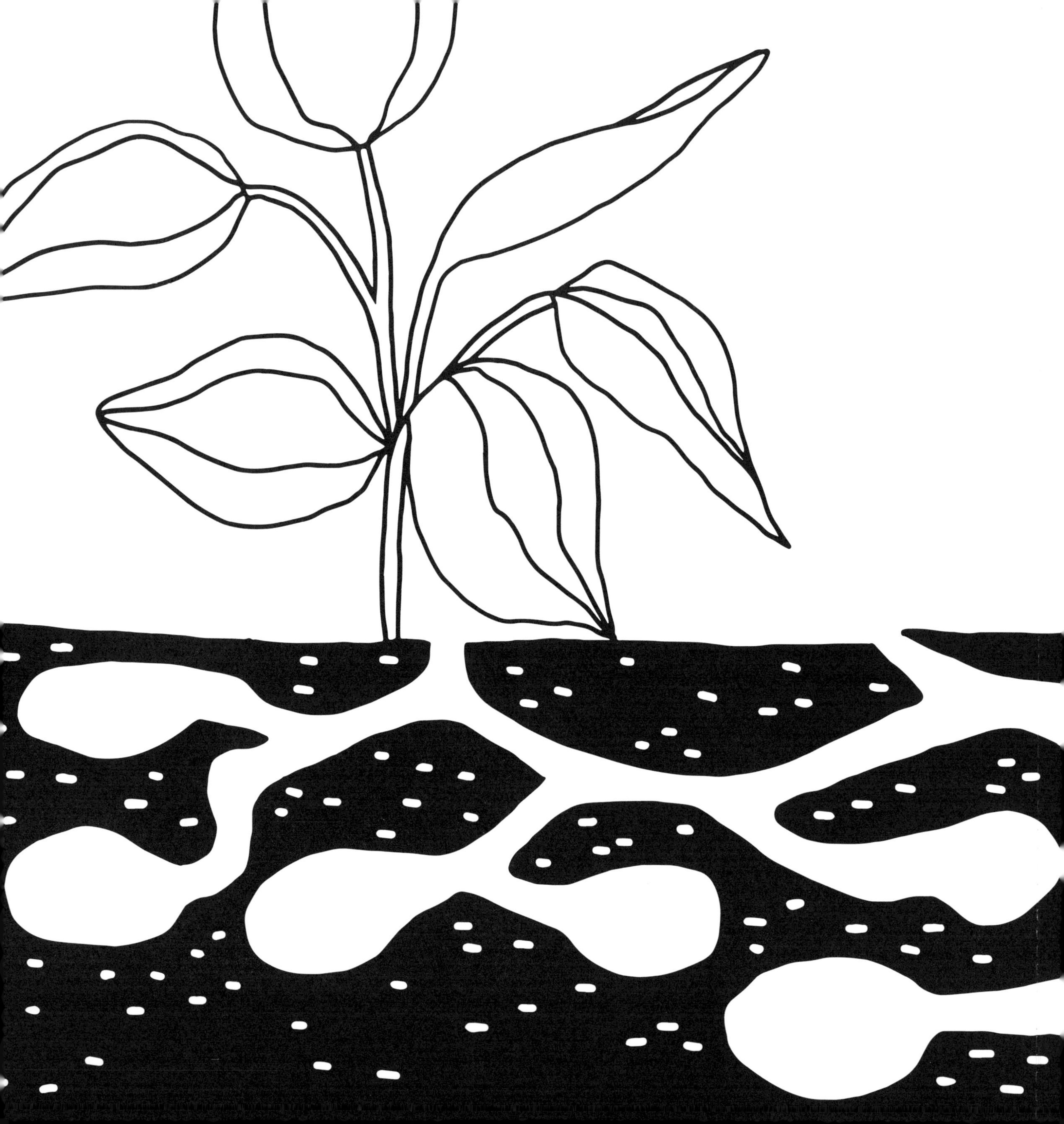

BUG THINGS

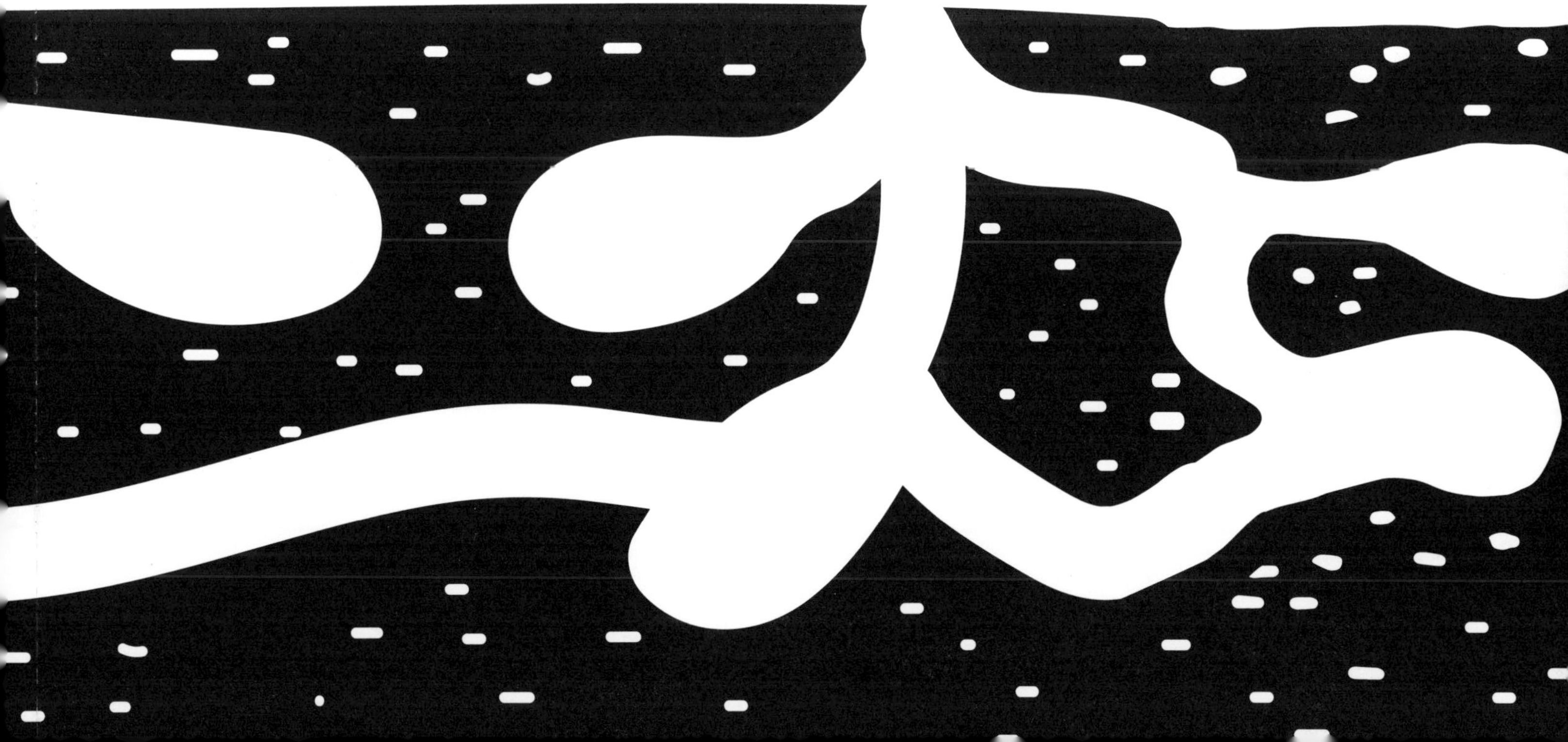

MAGNIFYING GLASS

A magnifying glass makes small things look huge. It bends light so you can see details you'd never notice with your eyes alone.

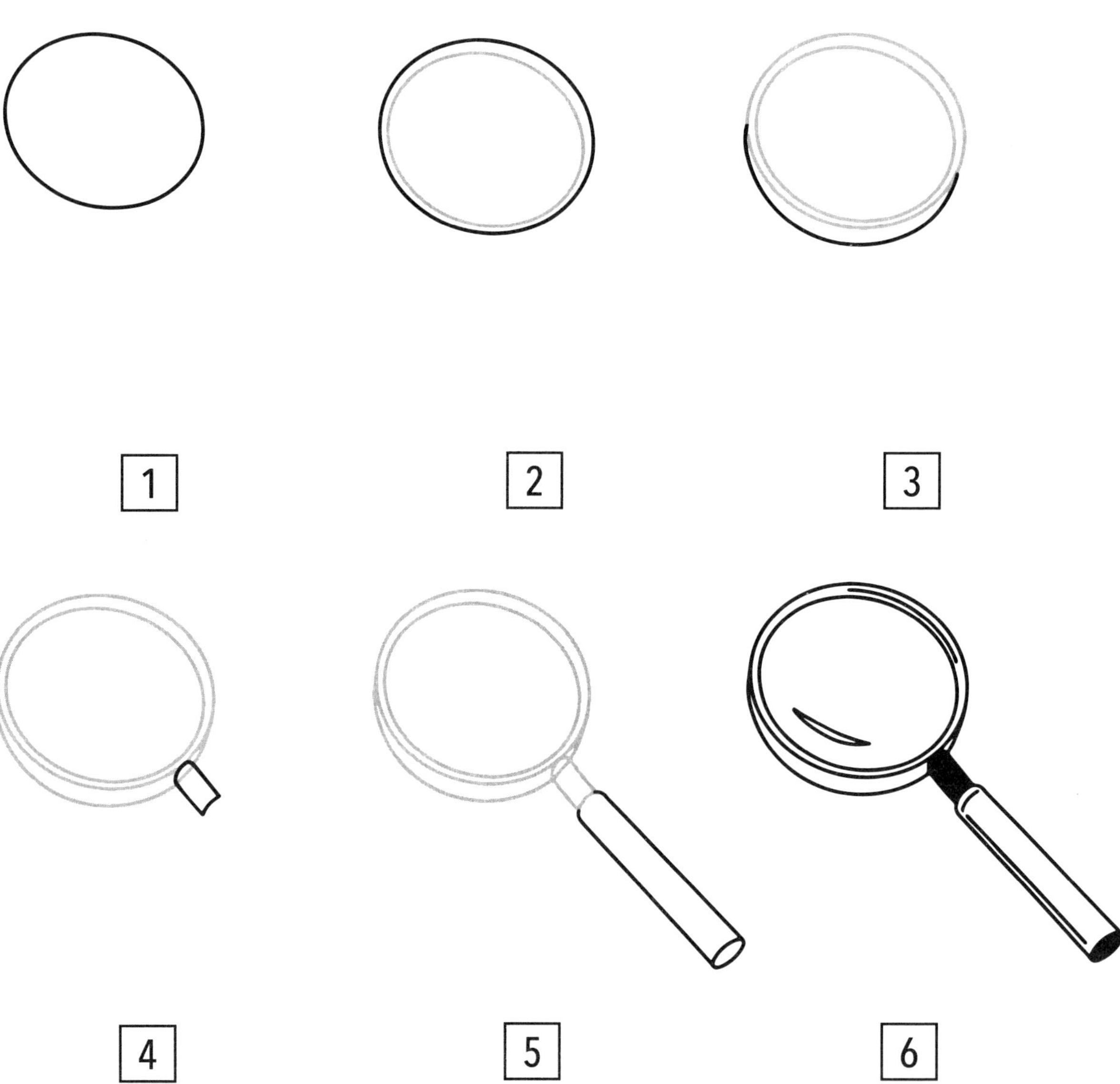

NET

A bug net helps people catch insects to look at up close. It's made of soft mesh that lets air through but traps bugs gently so they can be studied and released.

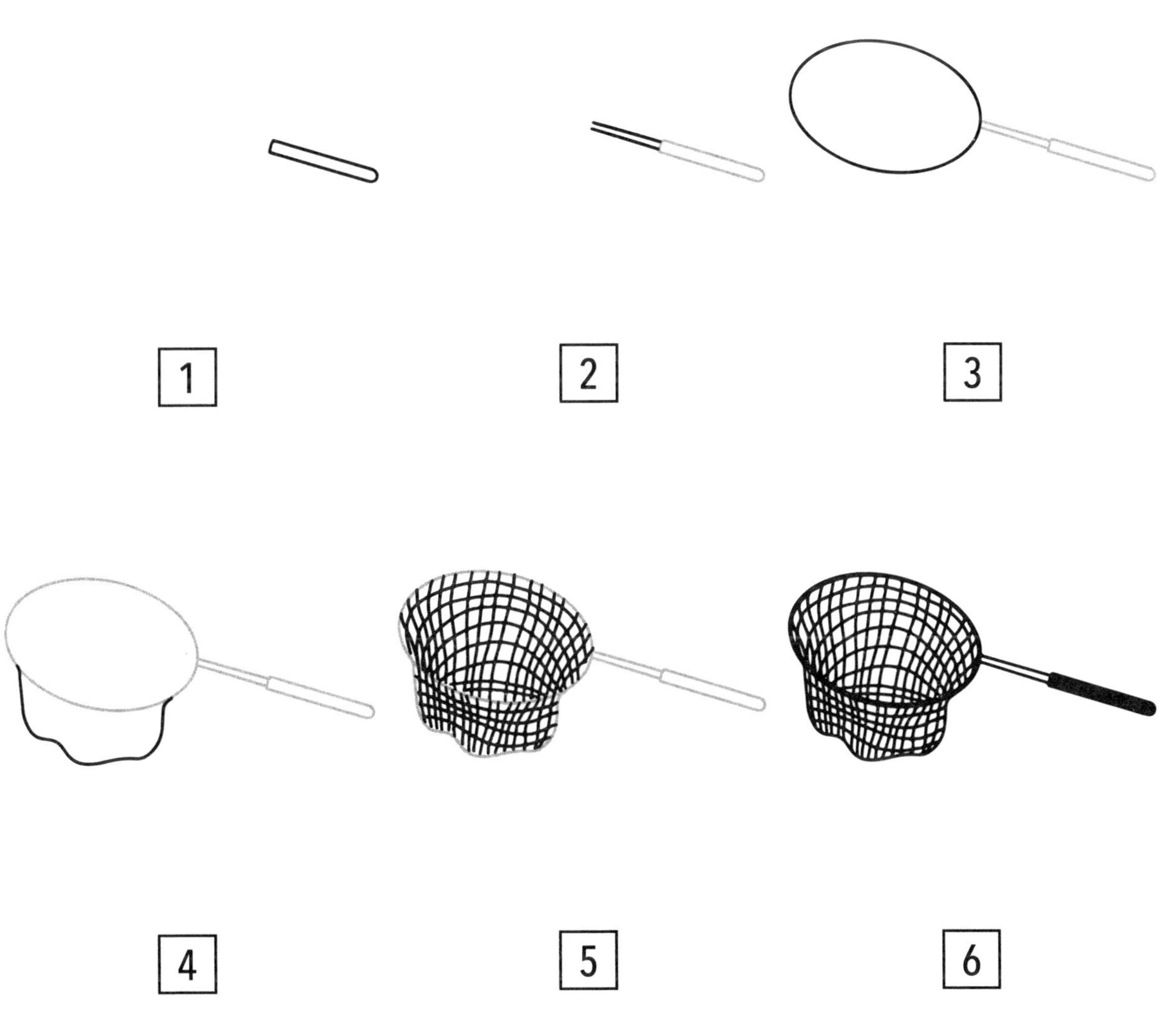

ANT FARM

Ant farms were invented in the 1950s so people could watch ants build tunnels and work together like a tiny city underground.

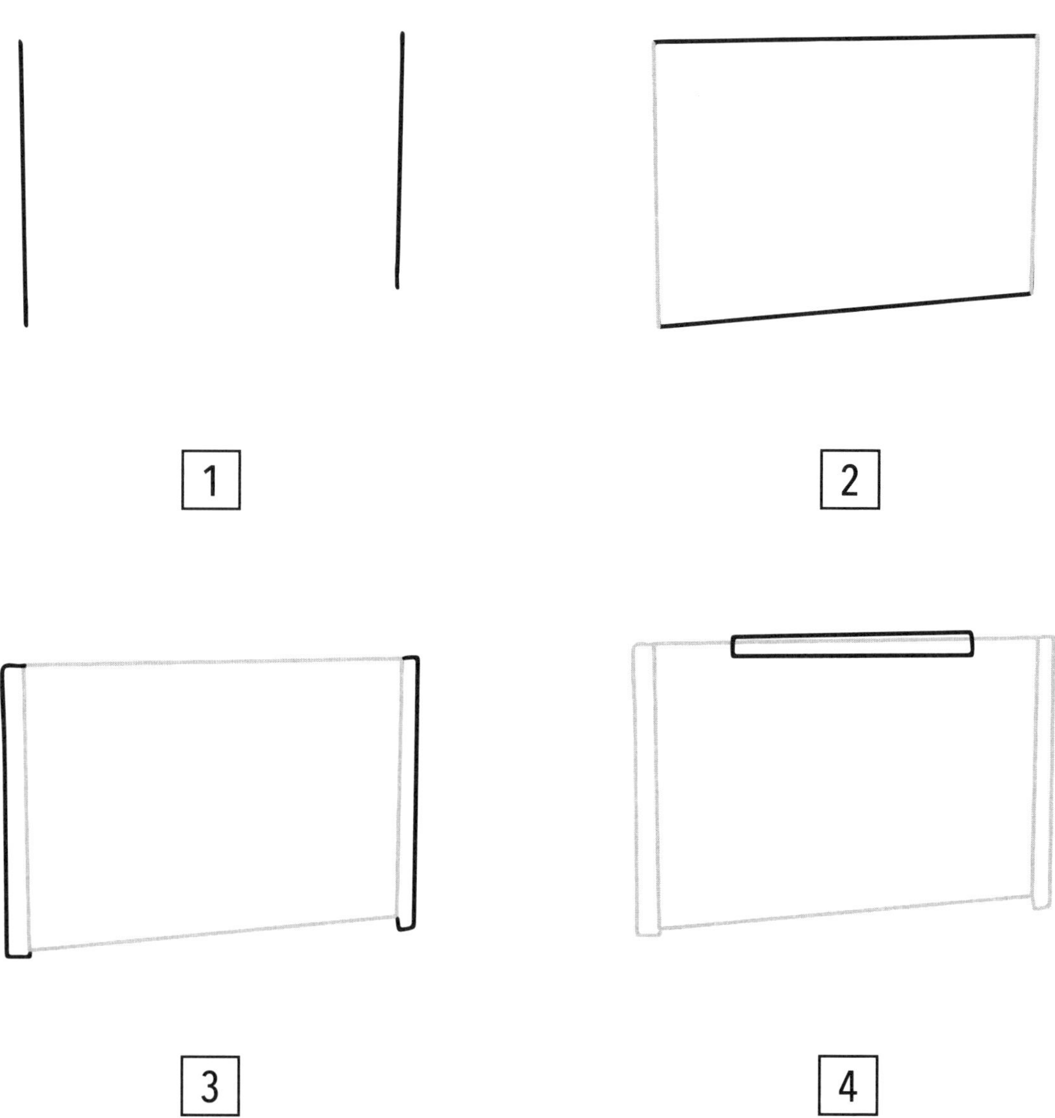

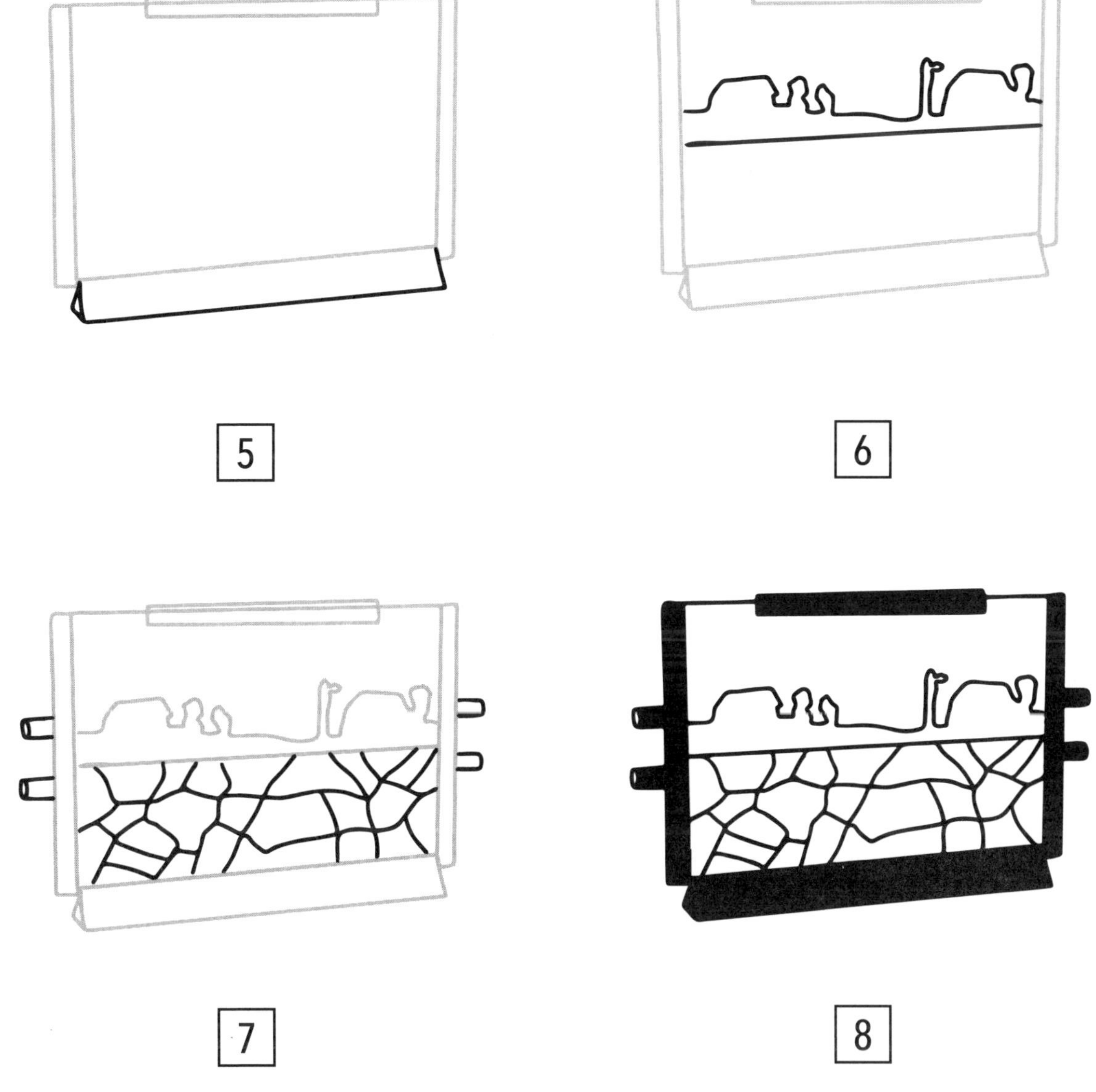

5
6
7
8

TERRARIUM

A terrarium is like a tiny rainforest in a jar and is perfect for watching beetles, roly-polies, or stick insects live in their own mini world.

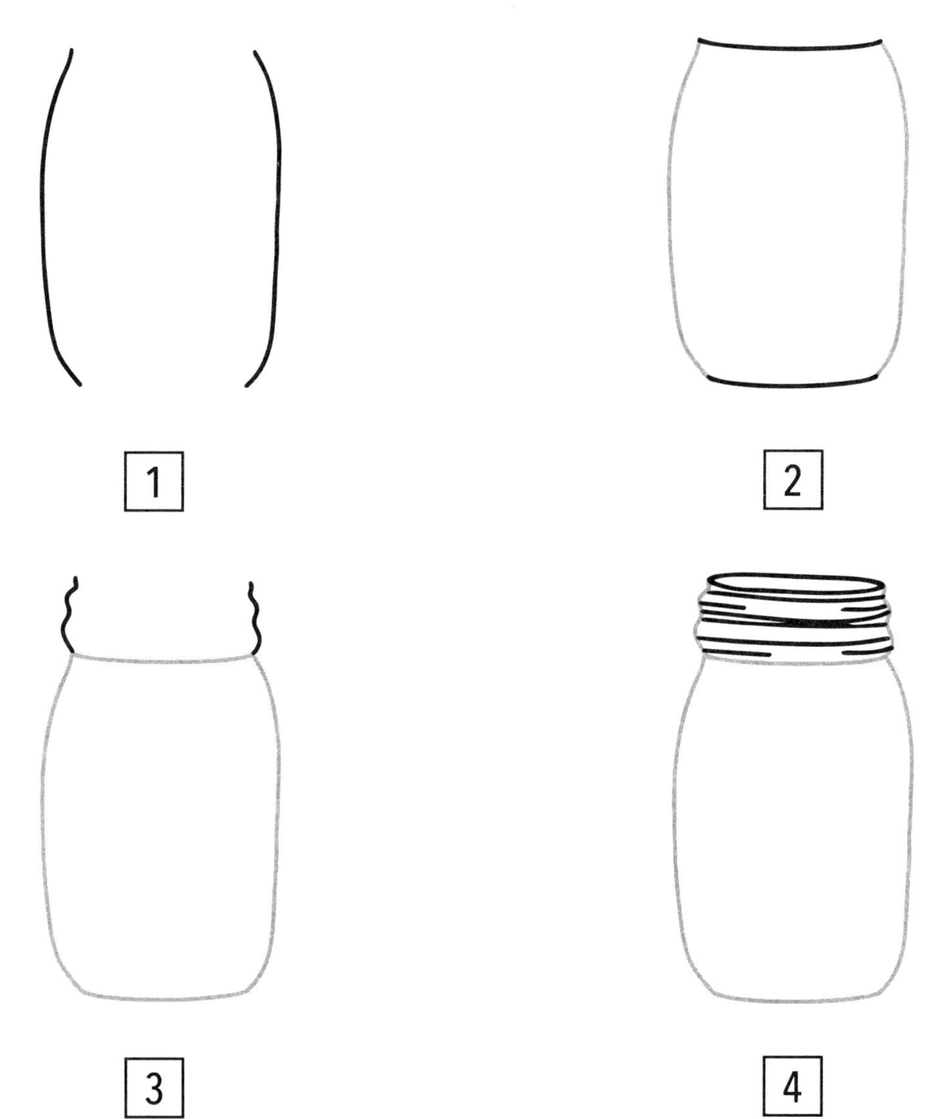

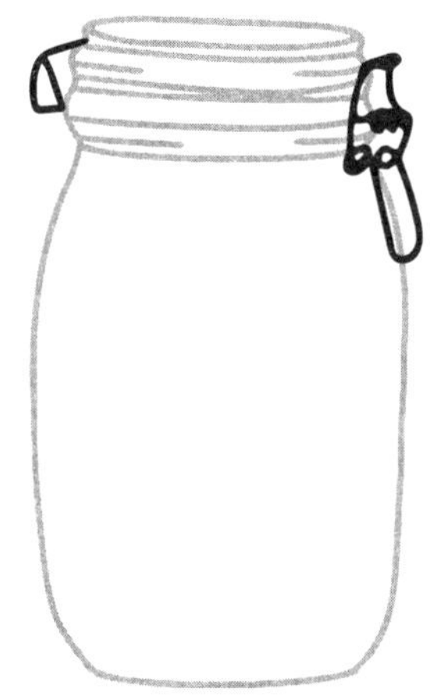

5

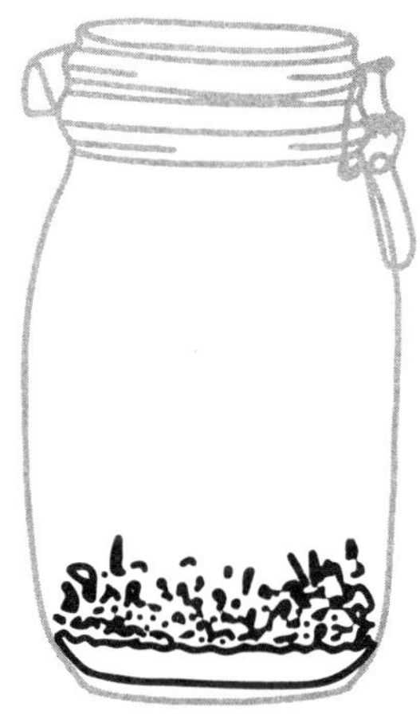

6

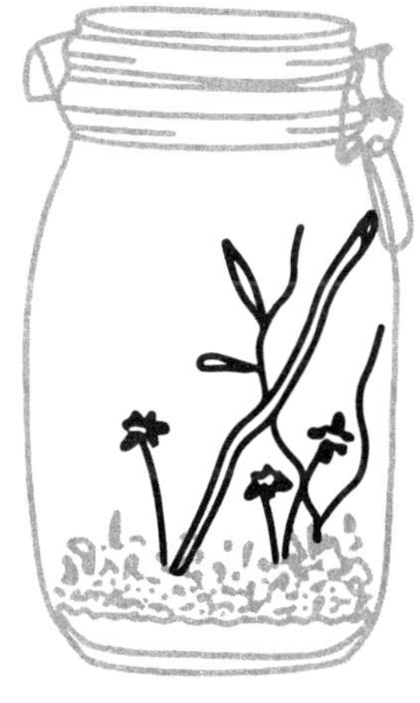

7

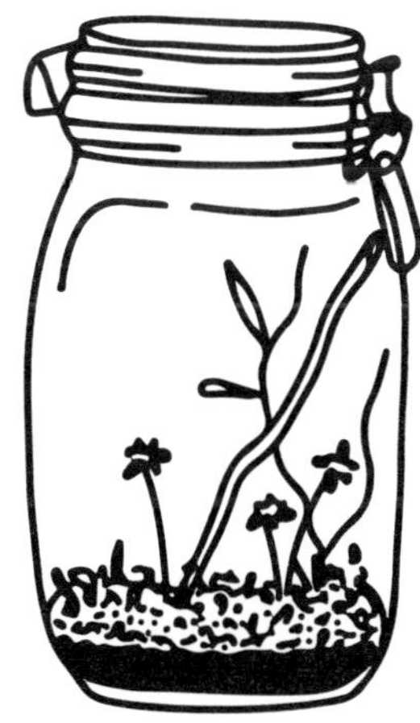

8

BEEKEEPER HAT

A beekeeper's hat has a protective veil made of mesh. It keeps stingers out but lets fresh air in.

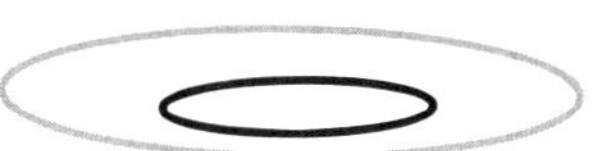

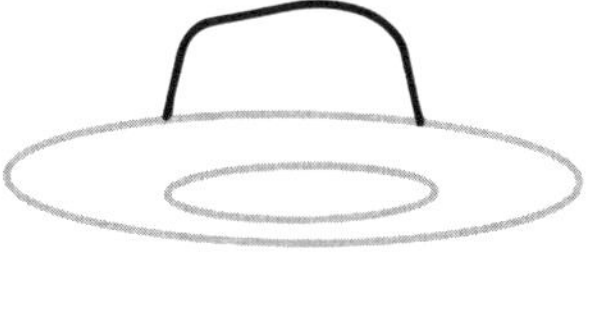

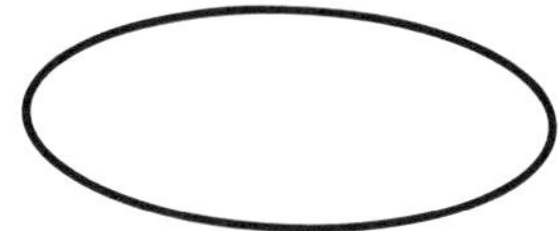

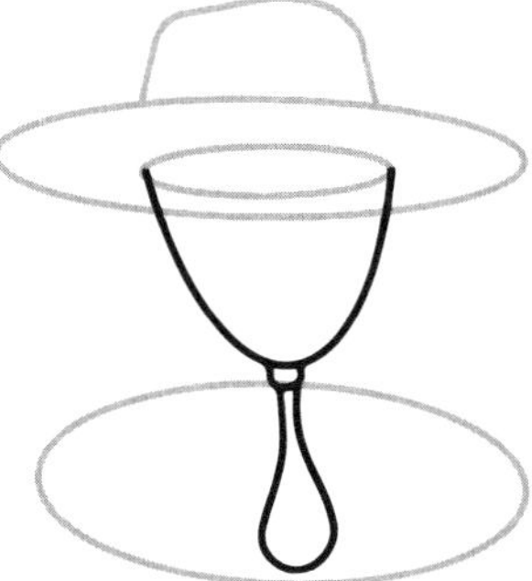

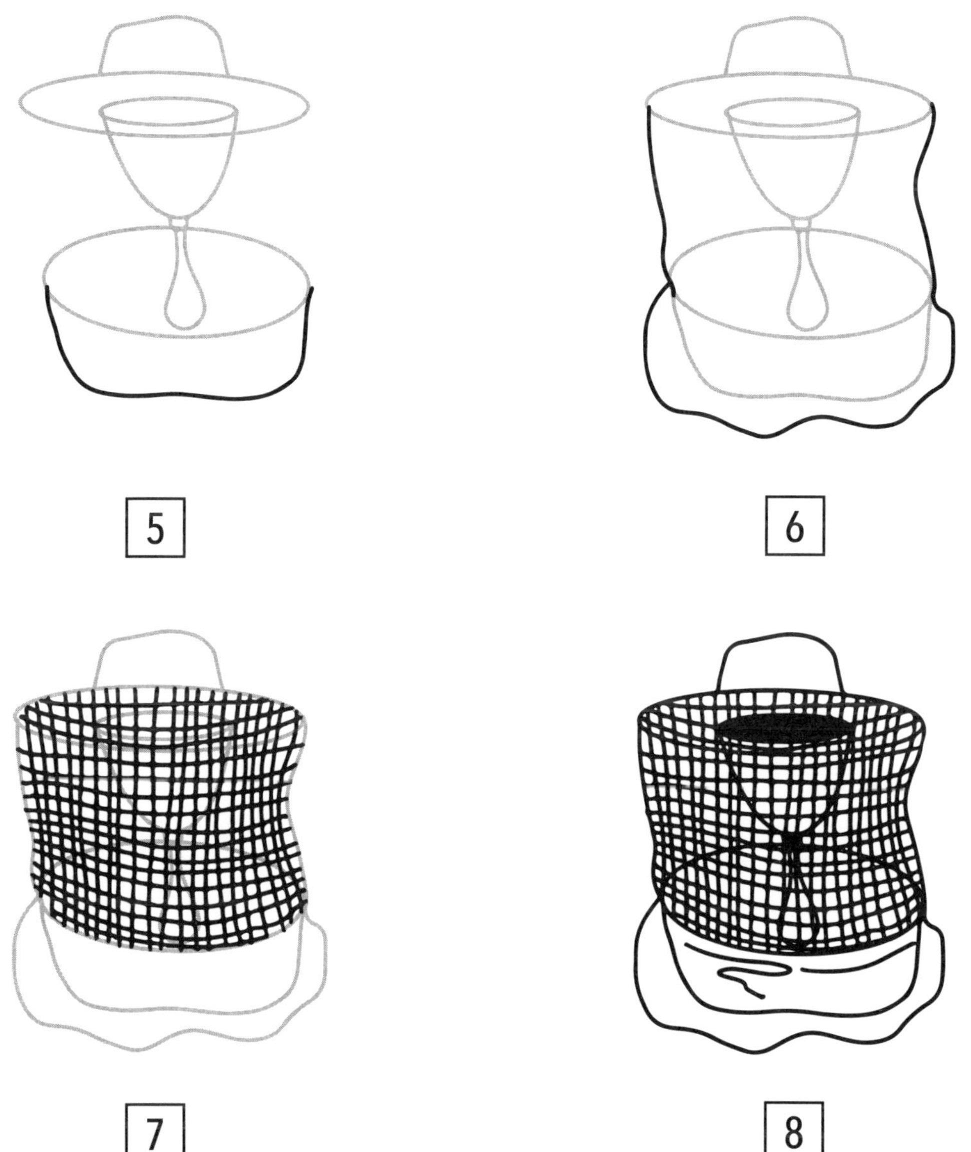

5
6
7
8

BEEHIVE

A single hive can hold tens of thousands of bees that, working together, can make up to 100 pounds of honey a year.

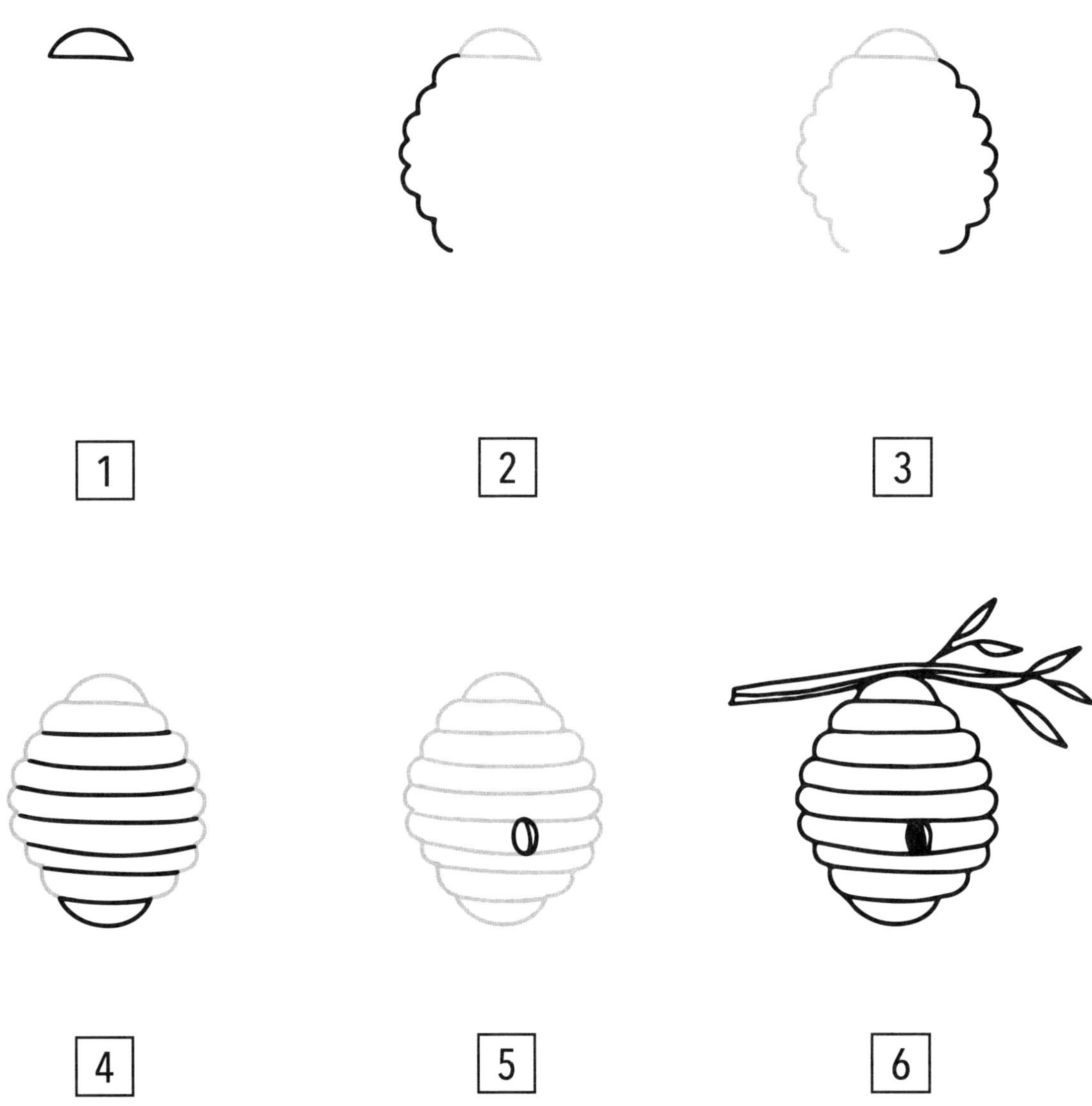

HONEYCOMB

Honeycomb is made by bees from wax they produce. Its hexagon-shaped cells store honey and pollen and provide a safe place for baby bees to grow inside the hive.

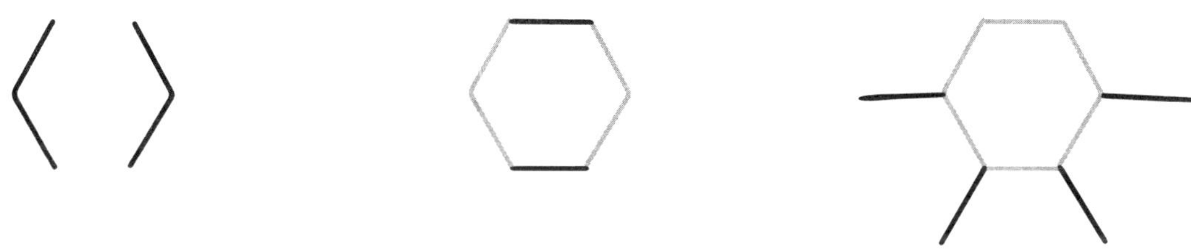

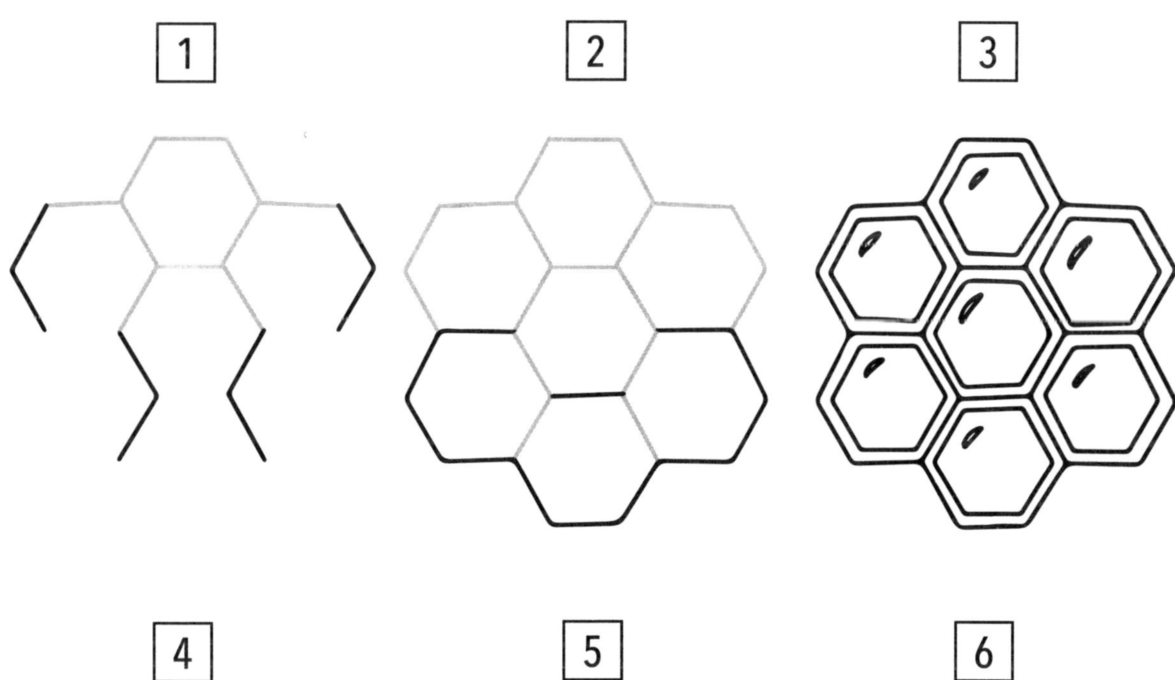

INSECT HOTEL

Insect hotels give bugs like bees, ladybugs, and beetles cozy homes.
They use the tiny holes and sticks to rest, nest, or hide from rain.

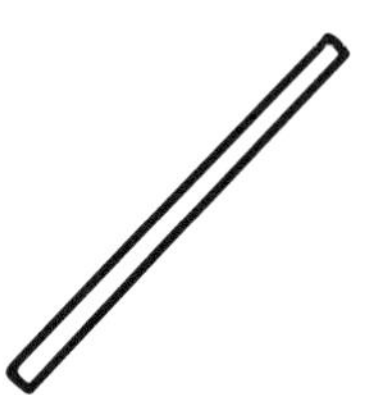

1

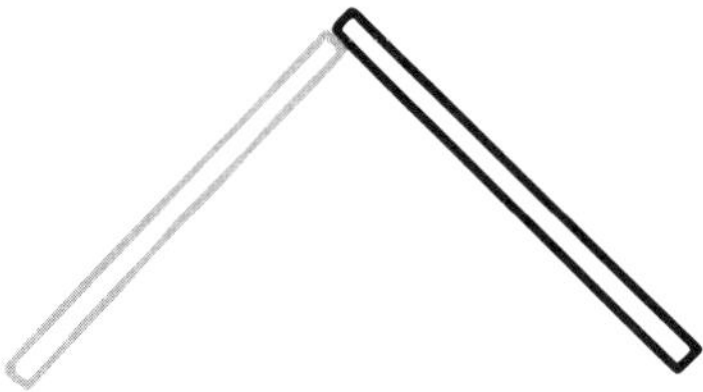

2

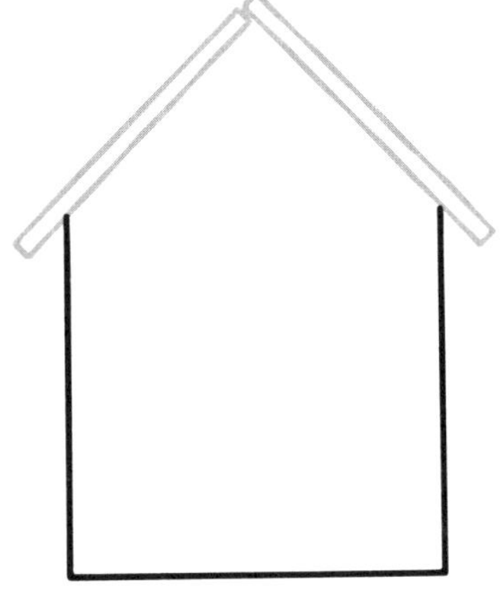

3

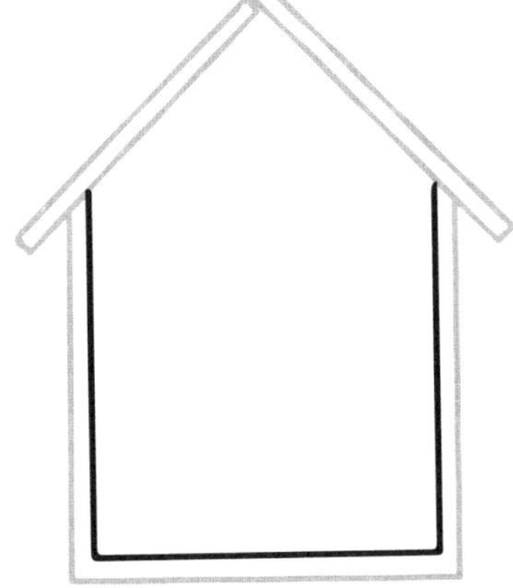

4

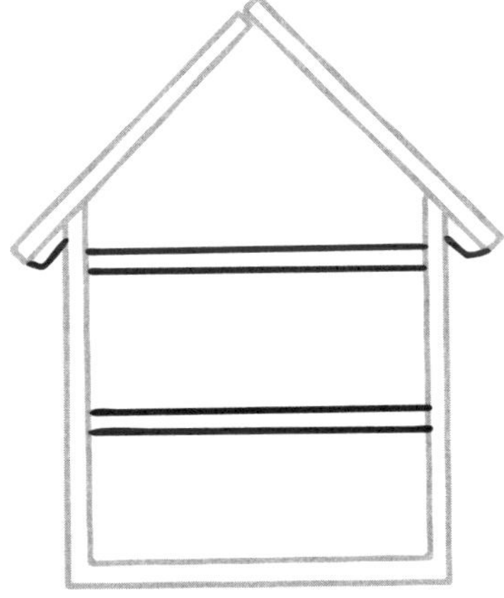

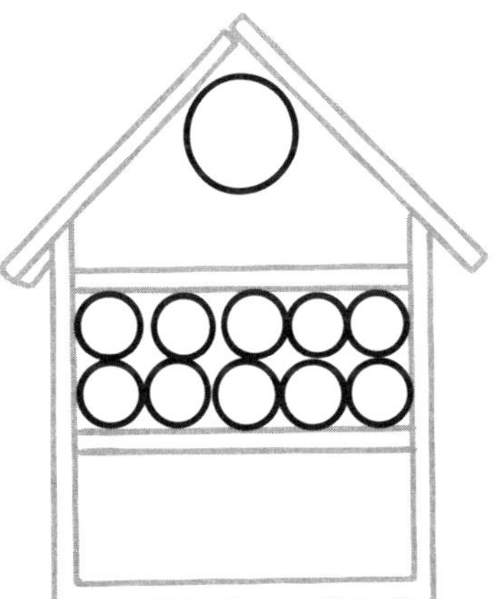

5

6

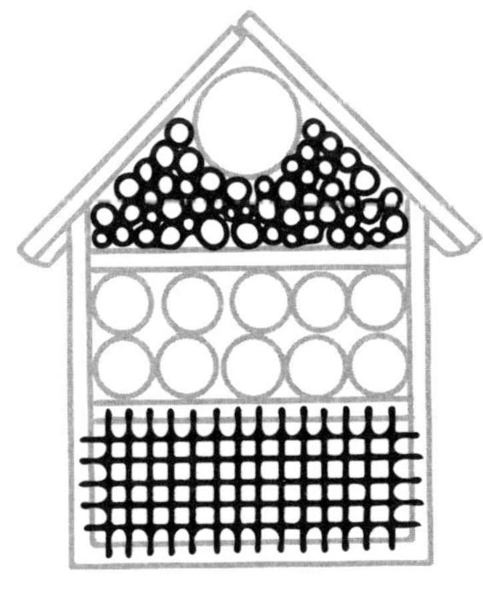

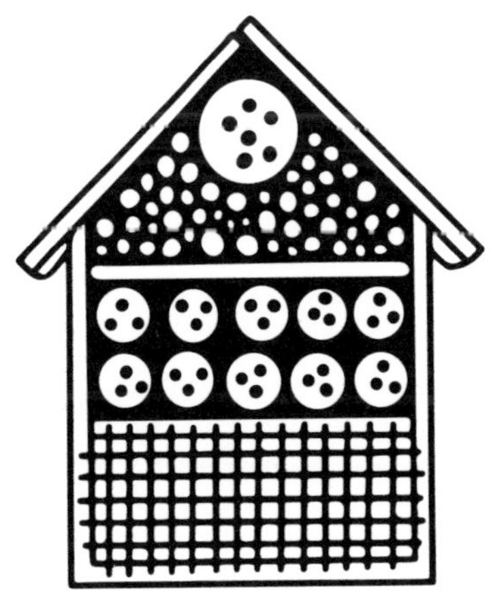

7

8

BUTTERFLY FEEDER

Butterflies help flowers bloom by carrying pollen from plant to plant.
A feeder filled with nectar helps them keep our world colorful and alive.

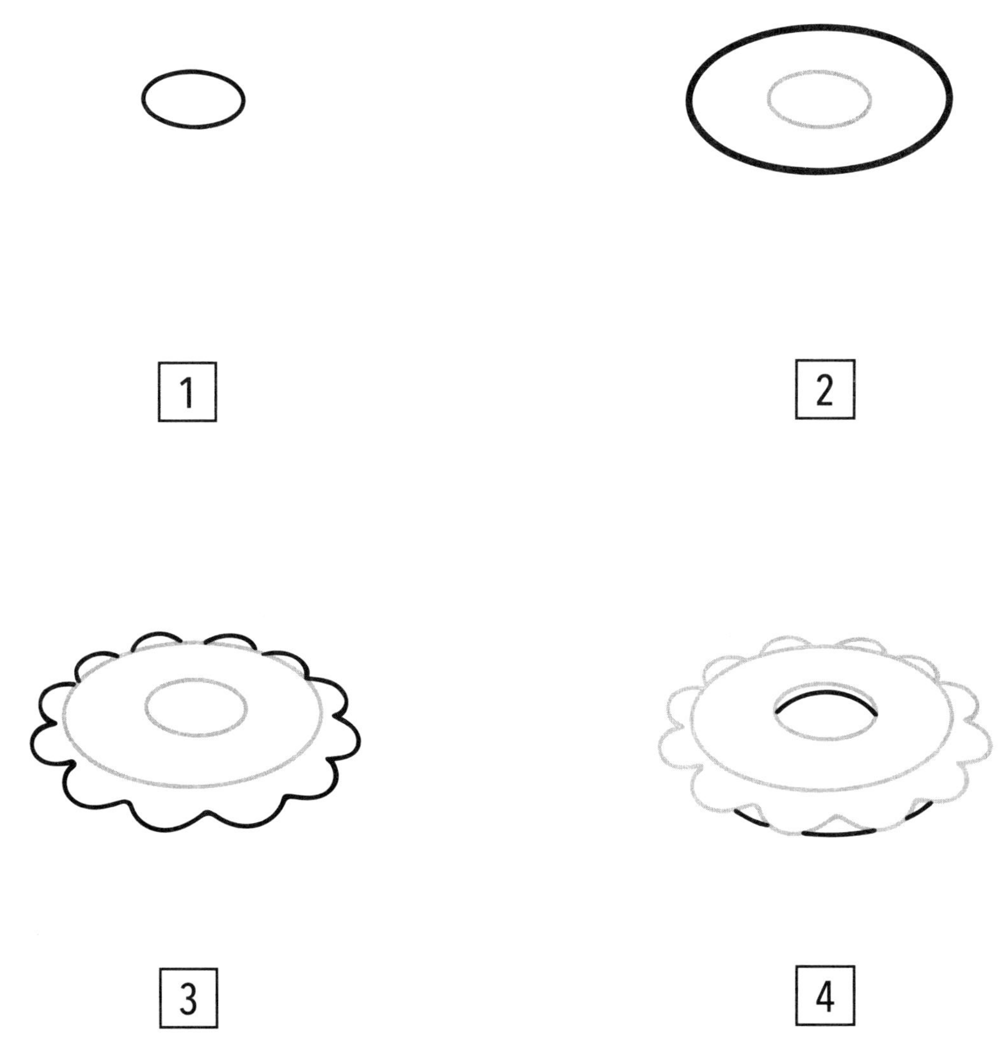

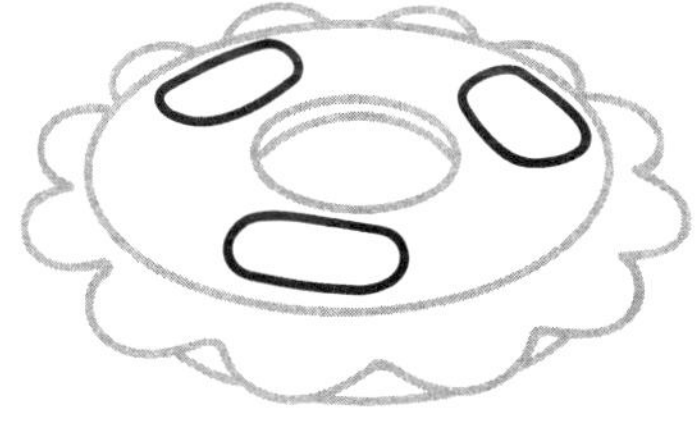

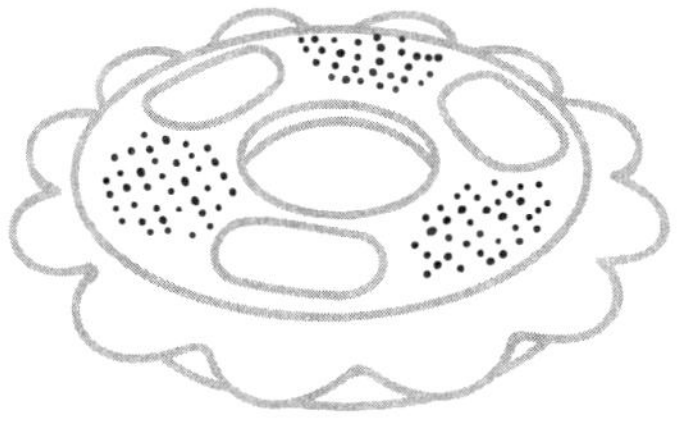

5

6

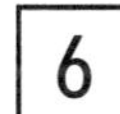

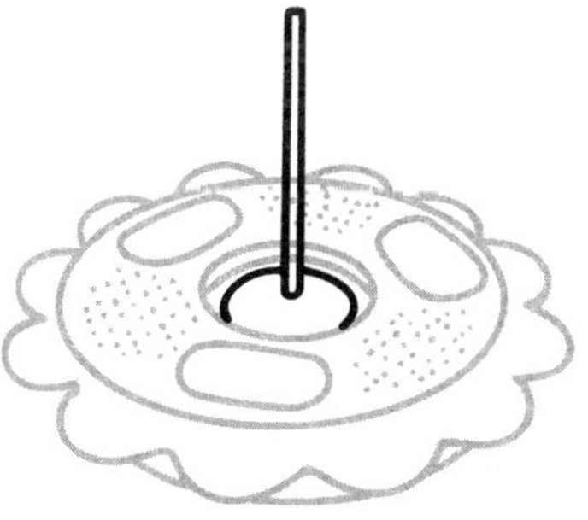

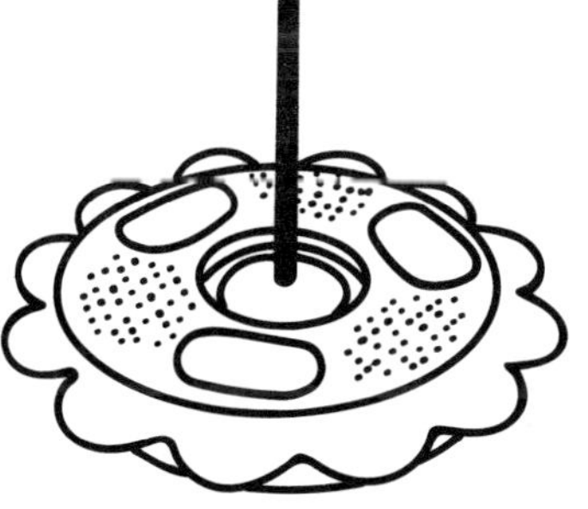

7

8

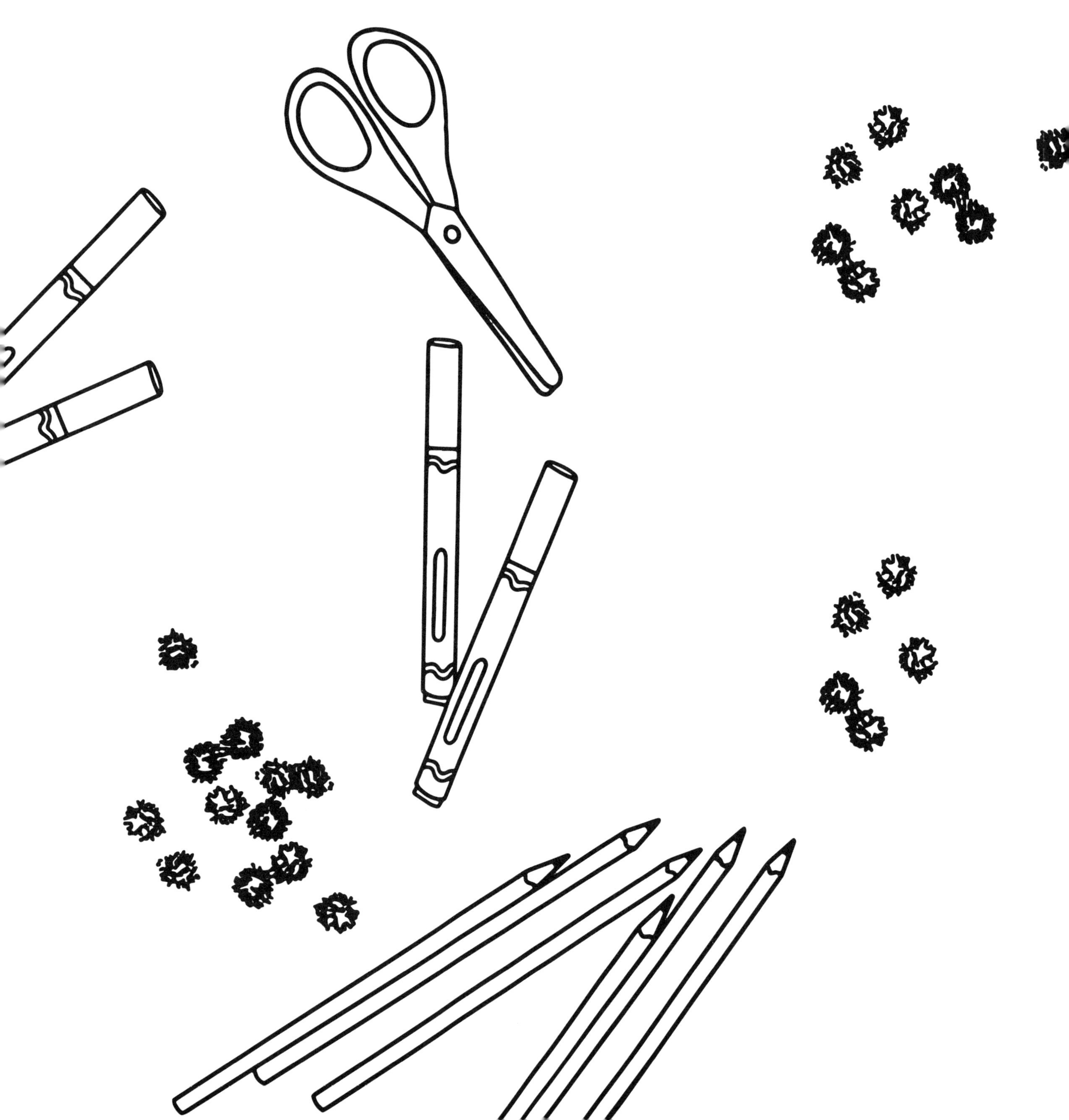

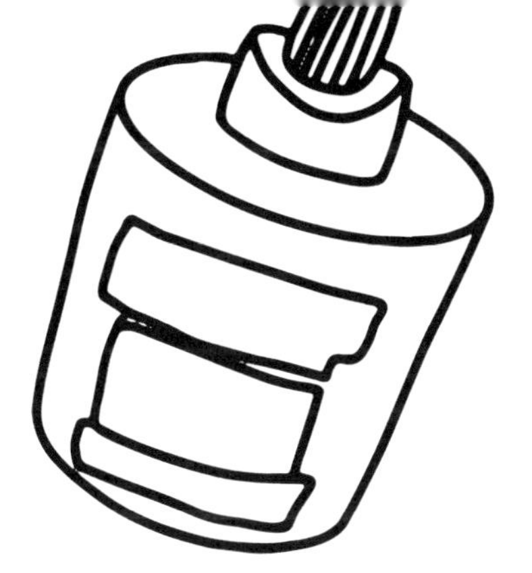

CREATE YOUR OWN

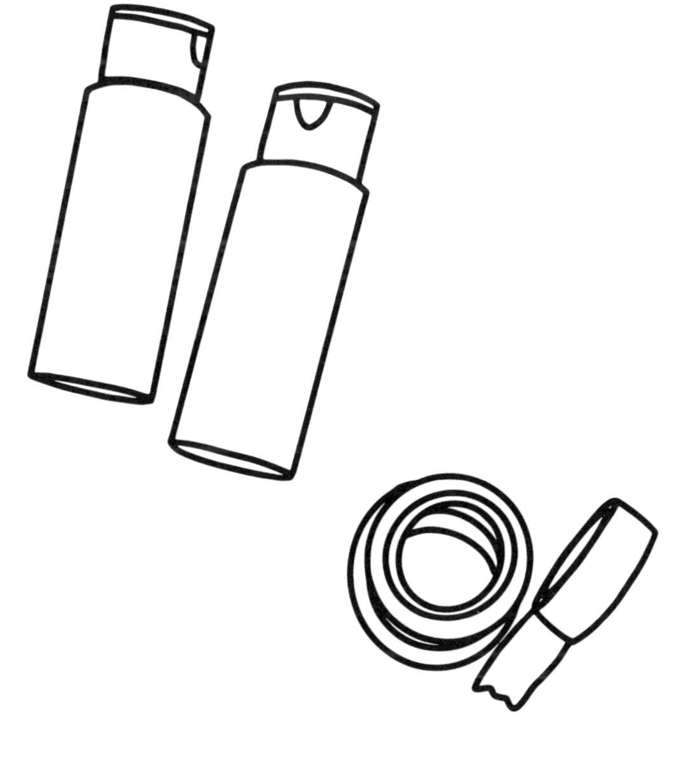

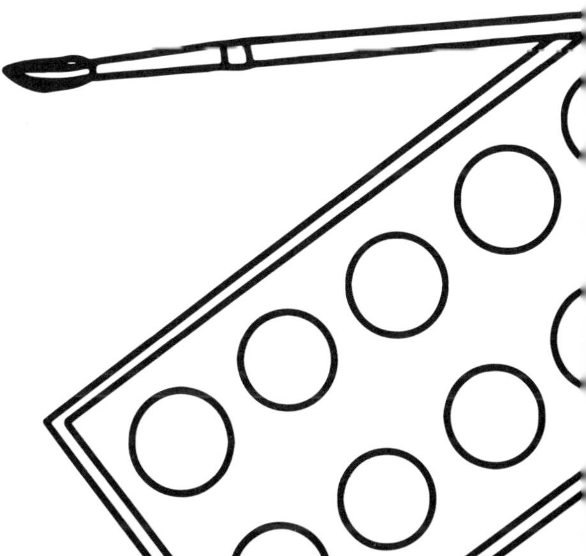

CREATE YOUR OWN TERRARIUM

Use this page to create a terrarium and fill it with what your bugs would like!

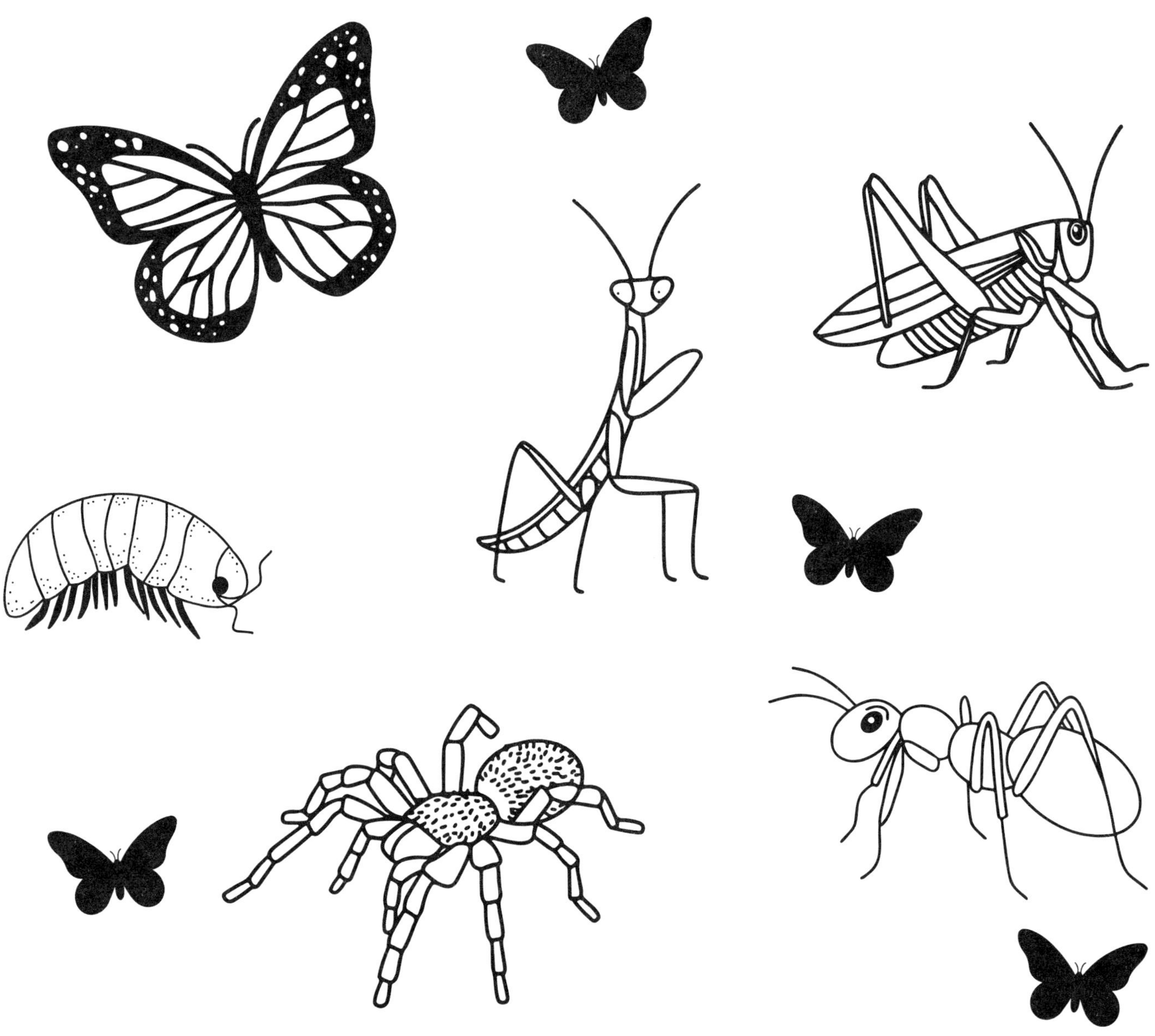

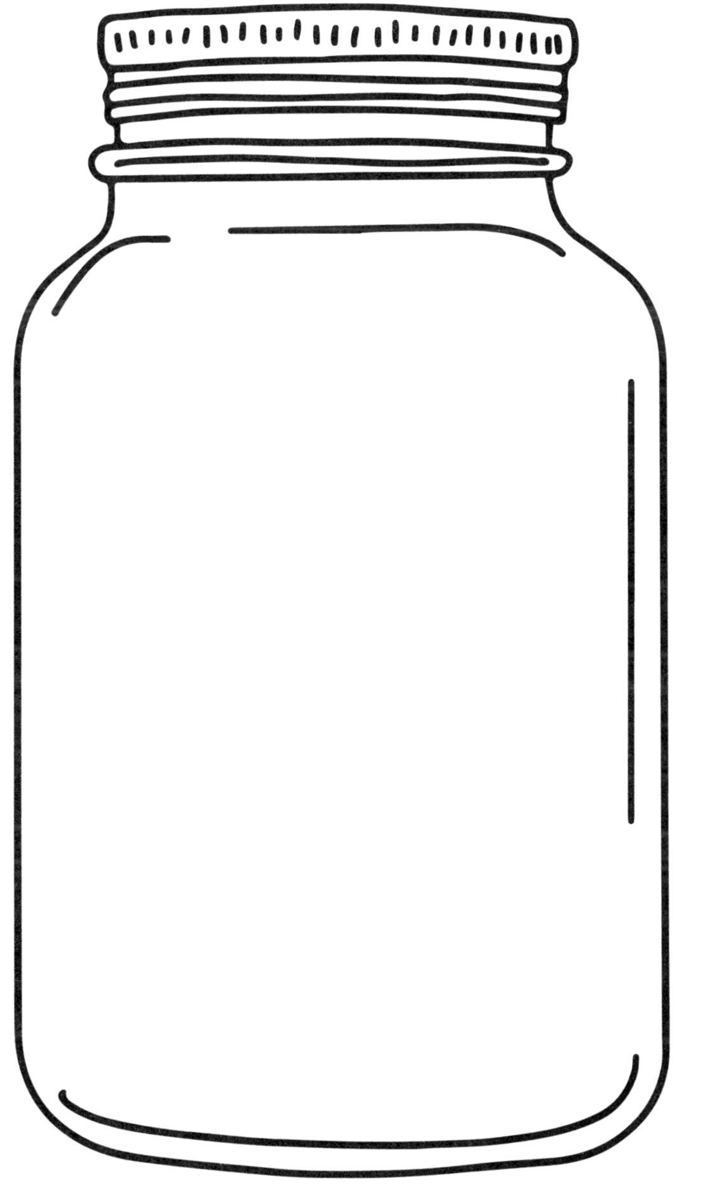

CREATE YOUR OWN INSECT HOTEL

Use this page to draw your own insect hotel!

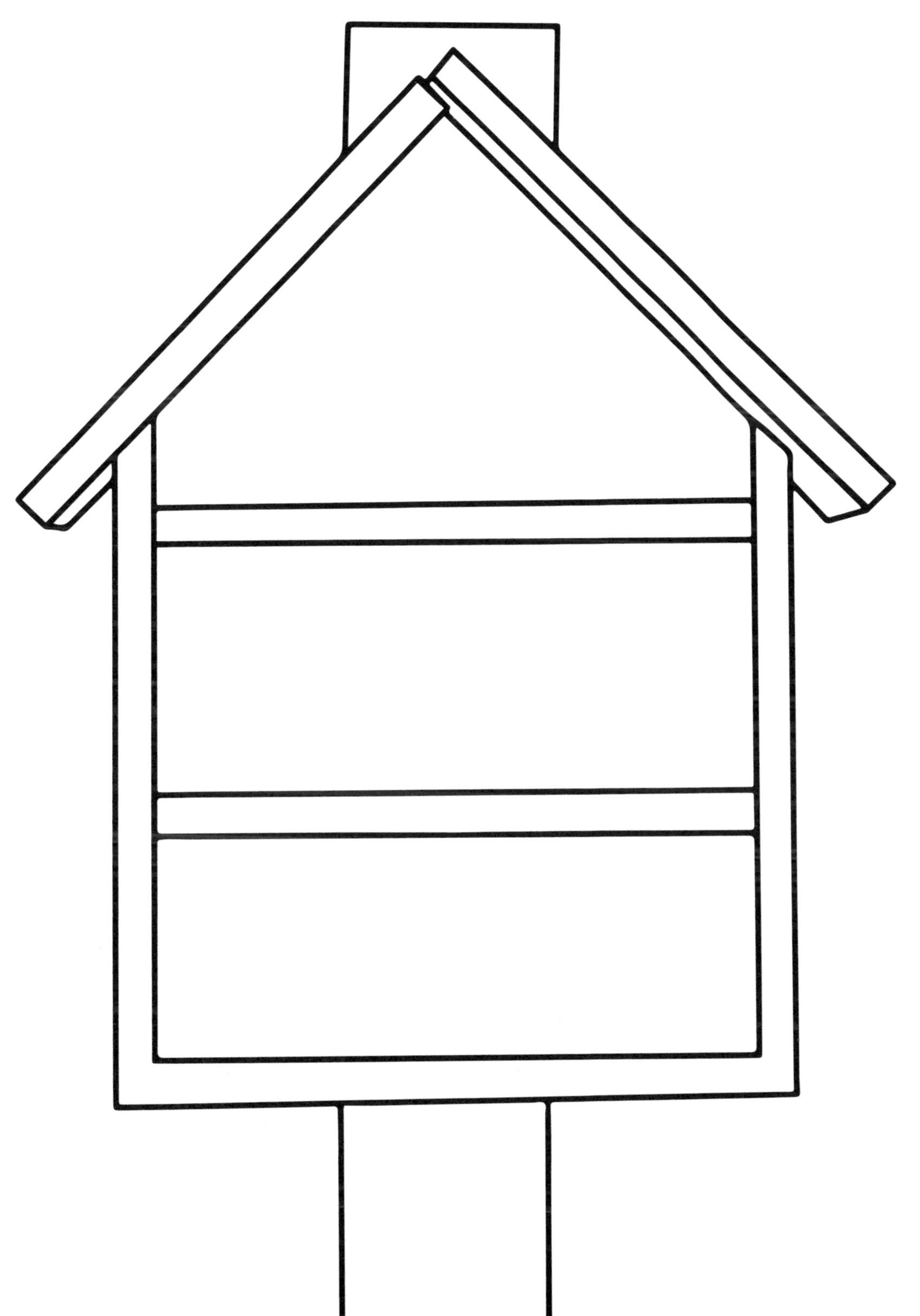

About Alli K

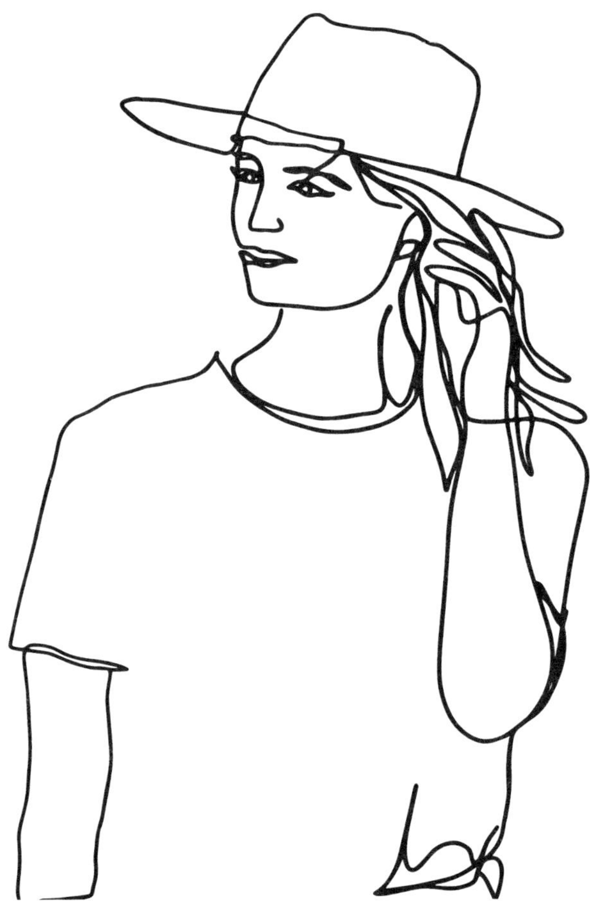

NAME: Alli Koch

HOME: Dallas, Texas

BIRTHDAY: March 20, 1991

FAVORITE COLOR: Black

FAVORITE BUG: Butterfly

JOB: I am a full-time artist! I sell my art online, paint murals on the sides of buildings, and teach others how to draw or be creative.

PETS: I have two cats named Emmie and Bex

CAR: Two-door Jeep

FAMILY: Married to my high school sweetheart

FAVORITE ANIMAL: Cats

FAVORITE THING TO DO: Play board games!

LOVE TO DRAW? COLLECT THE WHOLE *HOW TO DRAW FOR KIDS* SERIES!

- All the Things
- All the Magical Things
- All the Animals
- Modern Flowers
- Under the Sea
- Woodland Creatures
- Spring Things
- Summer Things
- Fall Things
- Winter Things